MEMOIR OF A WAR ON POVERTY IN PARADISE

By George Yokoyama

Published by Talk Story Press, 2015
Pepeʻekeo, Hawaiʻi
www.talkstorypress.org

Memoir of a War on Poverty in Paradise
Memoir
ISBN 978-0692353424
© 2015 George Yokoyama
All rights reserved

On the cover:

The price of a fishing rod that helps put food on the dinner table year-round is equal to the cost of buying fish for a single family dinner.

Painting by Kay Yokoyama

To my sister, Kay Yokoyama
And to my thousands of comrades in the war on poverty

Table of Contents

Chapter 1. The Formative Years of a Conviction 1
Chapter 2. A New Start 5
    In the Army Now 6
    Back Home 8
Chapter 3. Commitment to a Conviction 15
    Trouble at work 16
    Reorganization 20
Chapter 4. Politics is a Means to an End 21
    Youth Development Programs Impact Crime Rate 22
    Grant Writing 25
Chapter 5. Politics and Race Relations 27
    The Sprouting Buds of Politics 27
    First Governor's Campaign—Ariyoshi for Governor, 1974 29
    Youth Development Program 32
    Race Relations Project 33
Chapter 6. Trouble at Hilo High 37
    Locus of Control 39
Chapter 7. Daniel Akaka for Congress, 1976 41
    Dinner Disaster 45
    Mistakes Were Made 47
    Election Day, 1976 47
Chapter 8. Moving Forward 49
    Ariyoshi Re-election, 1978 50

Chapter 9. Community Action ... 55
　Vote of Confidence, 1980 ... 56
Chapter 10. Needing State Government Funds ... 59
　Day of Reckoning ... 64
　New Philosophy About Mobilizing Funds ... 65
Chapter 11. A Hawaiian for Lieutenant Governor, 1982 ... 67
　1982 Election ... 69
Chapter 12. Lull ... 71
　1984 Election ... 73
　Transportation Program Funding Cut ... 73
Chapter 13. The Advocacy and Power of the Press ... 77
Chapter 14. Waihee for Governor, 1986 ... 81
　Visiting Ka'u ... 84
　Grassroots Help ... 86
　The Next Generation ... 88
　Primary Day, 1986 ... 89
　Mobilization of Resources, 1986 ... 90
Chapter 15. Significant People ... 93
　Max Goldberger ... 94
　Larry Manliguis ... 96
　Other Individuals ... 97
Chapter 16. Reorganizing the Grassroots, 1988 ... 99
　1988: Dukakis for President ... 100
　Back Home and Choosing Candidates ... 103
　A Mover and Shaker ... 105
　Conflict in the Ranks ... 106
Chapter 17. Stepping Down ... 109
Chapter 18. The Domino Effect ... 115
Chapter 19. Opportunities ... 119
　Making Hay ... 120
　Jute ... 121
　Tour Boat Business ... 125
Chapter 20. Ben Cayetano for Governor, 1994 ... 131
Chapter 21. Cayetano's Second Term, 1998 ... 135

Chapter 22. Grants 141
    The Schedule 142
    Delay 144
    Worry 145
    The Projects 146
    What We Tried to Teach 149
    A Memorable Episode 152

Chapter 23. Harry Kim for Mayor, 2000 155

Chapter 24. Student Success 157
    Terror and War, 2001 158

Chapter 25. Governorship, 2002 161
    Lingle as a Strong Contender 163
    Success Stories 167

Chapter 26. More Funding 169
    Voices 171

Chapter 27. Elections of 2006 173

Chapter 28. Conniving at Head Start 177
    Trouble 177
    Repulsive Consequences of Living by the Political Sword 179
    Findings 184
    Mobilizing the Resources 186
    The Humiliation 191

Chapter 29. My Last Political Hurrah 195
    In My Honor 197
    Dr. Abercrombie 199
    Business Participation 201
    Visiting Miloli'i 202
    Meeting with the Grassroots 203
    The Big Day, 2010 205

Chapter 30. The Media, Unions, and Others 207

Chapter 31. The Hawaiians 211
    Sovereignty Bill 213
    The Input 214

Chapter 32. Politics and The Future 217

Epilogue 221

"Big Island's George Yokoyama makes big ripples in pond."

by Richard Borreca, Honolulu Star-Advertiser, July 16, 2010

The give-away was the aloha shirt hanging two inches below the bottom of the faded "Members Only" jacket.

It was during my first trip to Washington as a reporter.

Next to me in the U.S. Capitol elevator was a tiny man wearing a ball cap so big it rested on his ears.

"You from Hawai'i," I asked.

"Yup, I'm George," answered George Yokoyama.

"Got to see Akaka," he explained as he scurried out of the elevator, cupping a cigarette.

Yokoyama, 84, is one of those improbable delights that makes Hawai'i politics such a good story.

"George Yokoyama is one of the most real, interesting and unique people I ever met in Hawai'i politics or, for that matter, anywhere," says former U.S. Rep. Ed Case.

Case won Yokoyama's endorsement and support in campaigns for both governor and Congress, although when Case ran against Yokoyama's good friend U.S. Sen. Dan Akaka, Yokoyama went with the senator. Today Yokoyama is Neil Abercrombie's biggest Big Island supporter.

To his critics, Yokoyama as the 40-year-head of the Hawai'i County Economic Opportunity Council is one of the most flagrant Democratic Party ward heelers funneling government dollars into questionable projects.

His many supporters, who last night were to hold a roast honoring the retiring Yokoyama, point to more than $75 million in grant money that Yokoyama brought to the Big Island to develop projects ranging from raising bullfrogs to teaching seniors to use computers.

"He's the Pied Piper of economic development in the war against poverty," says Rep. Clift Tsuji, whom Yokoyama convinced to leave his job to run for a state representative seat in Hilo.

Politics and economic opportunity are all the same to Yokoyama and he approaches both with the verve and style of Hilo's version of Peter Falk playing Lt. Columbo.

"I first thought it had to be an act, but after you come to know him, you realize that he is doing it all from the heart. A lot of people believe George is one of the pivotal people on the Big Island," state Senate President Colleen Hanabusa says.

Noting that Yokoyama convinced Hawaiian activist Mililani Trask to endorse Case's run for governor, Hanabusa says, "When George calls out the troops, they come. He is an institution in Hilo."

While Hawai'i politicians are racing to embrace Twitter and Facebook to campaign, Case says that what they really need is the support of a grizzled veteran like Yokoyama.

"Voters are still getting most of the information on which they rely to make their voting devisions through traditional media and old-fashioned talk story at the poke counter at KTA Hilo," says Case.

"George is just one of those people whose ripples in the pond are larger and broader than most."

Reprinted with permission, courtesy Richard Borreca and the Honolulu Star-Advertiser.

Chapter 1. The Formative Years of a Conviction

In 1954, when I was twenty-eight years old, I lived at a U.S. military camp in northern Japan and worked as a fire chief for the Army. I was surprised one day when a Japanese firefighter asked me if I would meet with an elderly gentleman he called Sensei (Teacher). Sensei lived on the outskirts of the nearby town Hachinohe, the firefighter said, and he wanted to talk to me.

I had no idea what it was about, but I accepted the invitation and went to the man's home. A tall, slim, clean-shaven Japanese man with white hair greeted me at the entrance, and I was surprised when he welcomed me not with a customary Oriental bow, but with a Western-style handshake. He escorted me into his house where we each sat on a *zabuton* (cushion) upon the *tatami* mat. He had a bamboo stick lying on the floor next to him. I was curious about why I was there.

And I was astonished, when he spoke, to hear a clear tenor voice speaking perfect English with a slight British accent.

"I apologize for taking the liberty of making an inquiry about you," he said.

He had read in the local newspaper that the Kikyono village mayor gave me a medal of appreciation after I prevented the village from being destroyed by fire during a severe windstorm. He told me he also noted that my being in charge of fire stations that were manned by more than one hundred firefighting personnel in U.S. Army installations within the Aomori Prefecture demonstrated my leadership qualities.

"But I am most interested," he said, "to learn that you were born and raised in the territory of Hawaiʻi. All of this is why I asked for this meeting."

He had retired from the Ministry of Foreign Affairs many years ago, before the war, and moved to northern Japan during relentless wartime air raids that destroyed his home in Tokyo.

He told me he was ninety-four years old and that as his time on Earth neared its end, he needed to express his emotion, which he had repressed for years, about the inhumanely cruel overthrow of the Hawaiian nation. The overthrow had, he said, instantly imposed an unfamiliar and unwanted U.S. citizenship upon Native Hawaiians.

I interrupted. "The Hawaiian nation was very fortunate to have been annexed by the United States. In elementary school, I learned that the Republic of Hawai'i requested the annexation."

He glared at me and slammed his bamboo stick down hard on the tatami mat. He told me that at least Japan—notwithstanding its devastation by atom bombs, its millions that died during the war, and the country's acceptance of an imposed, unconditional surrender—had remained a sovereign nation.

"Not the Hawaiian nation!" He spoke loudly. "Its overthrow was caused not by a war but came from within. It came about because of treachery instigated by non-Hawaiian businessmen who established a provisional government and then by the Republic of Hawai'i. And then the island nation's annexation by the United States was complete."

He was both appalled and disappointed at how ignorant I was of Hawaiian history. He implored me to understand that although the eloquent Declaration of Independence and the Constitution were established for citizens of the United States, they implied a universal right of men that extended to all people.

He told me that the United States had violated—both in principle and spirit—the doctrines of equality of men, and civil rights and justice for all. He said that when it came to the overthrow, the United States did not practice what it preached.

His monologue went on for more than two hours, and I regret that I only remember a bit of what followed. I am even more embarrassed that I don't know his real name, because when we were introduced he was only referred to as Sensei, and because of my indifference at the time.

I do recall that he told me he lived through the Meiji Restoration of 1868. That's when the rule of the Shogunate ended and a new Japan emerged, with, at its helm, the young Emperor Meiji, who proclaimed by imperial edict that his people should seek knowledge from throughout the world to contribute to the modernization of Japan. In obedience with that edict, Sensei's father, a former *samurai* and high-ranking government official, hired a private English tutor for Sensei to learn English while still a child.

When Sensei was a teenager, the government selected him to study abroad, first in England and later in California, where he befriended a young fellow student from Hawai'i. They talked endlessly about the similarities and differences in life between Hawai'i and Japan, and pledged to reciprocate visits in order to promote a friendly relationship between the countries.

Upon returning to Japan from abroad, Sensei was assigned to the Ministry of Foreign Affairs. He felt honored to be selected as one of the top interpreters for King Kalākaua's visit to Japan during the Hawaiian king's 1881 tour around the world.

Sensei told me that while he was interpreting for the King he committed a breach of protocol: He spoke unofficially, and told the king that while studying in California he had befriended a Native Hawaiian of nobility. Kalākaua knew the young Hawaiian, Sensei's friend; it was a relative he had sent to California to study. The king was impressed with Sensei's ability to speak English and invited him to visit Hawai'i. Sensei was elated by the king's response, even despite his breach of etiquette.

> In 1881, King Kalākaua traveled around the world to study immigration, improve foreign relations, and see how other rulers ruled. His first stop was San Francisco, where he received a royal welcome. He continued on to Japan where he met with the Meiji Emperor. Then he went on to Qing Dynasty China, and then to what was then Siam, Burma, British Raj India, Egypt, Italy, Belgium, the German Empire, Austria-Hungary, the French Third Republic, Spain, Portugal, the United Kingdom of Great Britain and Ireland. He traveled through the United States before returning to Hawai'i. He was the first king to travel around the world. On his journey, he met with many other crowned heads of state, including Pope Leo XIII, Umberto I of Italy, William I of Germany, U.S. President Chester A. Arthur, and Queen Victoria. William N. Armstrong, a member of the King's Cabinet who accompanied the king, wrote about the trip in the book *Around the World With a King*.

He wrote to his Hawaiian friend about his encounter with the king and promised that someday he would visit Hawai'i. In the meantime, though, Kalākaua passed away, and his sister, Lili'uokalani, ascended the throne. It was during her reign that the Hawaiian nation was overthrown, and Hawai'i became a territory of the United States.

Finally, in the early 1900s, Sensei was selected to visit Hawai'i on a diplomatic mission. But, sadly, the islands were no longer the Hawai'i he dreamed of. Gone were the pomp and splendor of a paradisiacal kingdom inhabited by a warm and friendly people, he said. Above all else, the young Hawaiian student he had befriended had passed away.

He concluded his heartfelt story by begging me, earnestly and humbly, to be kind, respectful and helpful to the Native Hawaiian people when I returned to Hawai'i. Then he sighed in relief, smiled for the first time, and thanked me for being a good listener. I departed with a handshake, knowing that due to his age, I was unlikely to ever see him again.

I regret that he never knew how much his words affected me. I always kept close my memories of this encounter with Sensei—who was, indeed, my teacher—and in fact his words defined much of the work I did in my long career.

Chapter 2. A New Start

I was born in Hilo in 1926 and lived there until I was seven years old, when my mother took my two sisters and me to Japan. We lived with her parents in Japan for two years, and that's where I attended first and second grade.

When we returned to Hilo, my mom enrolled me at Hilo Union Elementary School where they discovered I'd forgotten how to speak English. At first they put me in kindergarten, so I could learn the language again, and then after several months, they moved me up to first grade. I relearned English by speaking Pidgin with my friends at school. That's the strength of being bilingual. If you don't know how to say it in one language, you can translate it into another.

I remember all of my Hilo Union teachers through those important, formative years. In first grade, it was Mrs. Goo and in second grade, Mrs. Kim. Third grade was Mrs. Maneki, fourth grade was Mrs. Shaughnessy, and fifth grade, Mrs. Ludloff.

My favorite teacher was Mrs. Chock, who taught sixth grade at Hilo Union School, because she was the one who taught me how to study and about all the psychological instruction behind it. Not the classroom curriculum, but the non-curriculum stuff: the motivation, persistence and resiliency. The learning that if you fall down, you just stand up again right away. That's missing these days. Now they only teach the curriculum and the computer.

Mrs. Chock really taught me independent thinking and learning, and I finally got the hang of it. I made the honor roll for the first time in the seventh grade.

World War II came to Hawai'i during my eighth-grade year. I went on to Hilo High, and I was bad in those days. One day there were six of us smoking back by the cafeteria when the principal walked up, and he nailed me.

I said, "What about the others?! They smoking too!"

He said, "No. You."

He brought me in his office and started lecturing me.

"America is at war with Japan," he said. "You are at war with Japan. You are Japanese, and you have to behave yourself. What you can do for your country is go into the Army and fight for your country."

A teacher had just said the same thing to me, and I didn't like it. That teacher had seen three textbooks lying on some steps near me and looked at me. I called out whose books they were, but the teacher pointed at them and told me to pick them up. I said they weren't my books; they were someone else's.

He said, "Come here." He took me on the side and said, "America is at war with Japan, and you are Japanese. These days, even with young Japanese kids, they report movements to the Japanese."

When I was in the principal's office and hearing the same thing, I didn't like it one bit.

I punched the principal, and then I walked out. There were two girls in the front office, but they didn't see me hit him. And he didn't do anything about it right away.

Two weeks later, though, I got a letter from the President of the United States. It said, "Welcome to the Army!" I learned that the principal was on the draft board. When he had problem students at his school, he sent them into the Army.

I didn't graduate from high school. That was 1945, and it was my junior year.

In the Army Now

I was approaching delinquency and had an "I don't give a damn" attitude when I entered the military. It turned out, though, that the army, with its strict adherence to a daily routine, its insistence on conformity and discipline, and its chain of command organizational structure, helped me tremendously as I became a young adult.

I was in Germany for four years, during Occupation there. From there I went to New York for another year, and then during the Korean War, I served in Korea for three months.

Then they dragged me to Japan, and I was there from 1952 until 1968, although I left the Army in December of 1955. I stayed in Japan because I took a civilian job with the U.S. Armed Forces as a fire chief; that's when I was in charge of fire protection at an Army installation on the outskirts of Tokyo.

I decided to go to school while I was in Japan. When people asked me about it, I told them that they could go, too, on the GI Bill. In those days, the GI Bill paid enough to live on.

I had a hard time getting into Sophia University there in Tokyo because I hadn't graduated from high school, but the dean was kind. Since I didn't have a diploma, he let me take a test, and I passed. He said we'd try it out and put me on probation for six months. It worked out.

It was a time when America was giving developing countries lots of money for economic development. And it was right after the Korean War, when there was a lot of surplus construction equipment being brought to a big depot in Japan and sold. My economics professor told me I could sell one bulldozer, and it would be the same as selling thousands of transistors, which were big then, so that's what I did. I bought big bulldozers and cranes and sold them to developing countries.

> The G.I. Bill (officially the "Servicemen's Readjustment Act of 1944") provided benefits for returning World War II veterans, commonly referred to as G.I.s. These included low-cost mortgages to buy a house, low-interest loans to start a business, tuition and living expenses for attending high school, college, or vocational school, and a year of unemployment compensation. These benefits were available to any veteran who had been on active duty for at least ninety days during the war years and who had not been dishonorably discharged. By 1965, about 2.2 million veterans had used G.I. Bill benefits to attend college and 6.6 million more for some type of training program.

It was going great until I got fleeced. I borrowed $200,000 from the bank to buy surplus jeeps, bulldozers, and cranes for this guy in the Philippines, shipped them all to him, and then he didn't pay. He took off and went to Vietnam instead. This was during the Vietnam War and there were crooks from all over the world taking advantage. In the jungles there was war, and in the cities there were all these crooked things going on.

Two hundred thousand dollars is a lot of money now, but fifty or sixty years ago! It was hard, but I paid back every cent of it. And then that was enough for me. I was over forty, and I didn't know what I was going to do next. My sister, Kay, told me to come back home to Hawai'i, so I did.

Back Home

I'd been away for twenty-three years and we were nearly penniless when my wife, Mieko, our three-year-old son, Paul, and I finally returned to my Hilo roots in January of 1968, and I was apprehensive and anxious about starting anew.

It would be an entirely new life. Kay and her husband, Richard, invited us to stay with them until I could find a job, and they gave us a used car so we were mobile. I got three part-time jobs: as an instructor at Hilo High School, as a lecturer teaching Japanese at the University of Hawai'i at Hilo, and as a legal assistant to an attorney.

One day I had a rather unbelievable encounter at the downtown Hilo post office. There stood a tall, slim, familiar figure dressed in black with a white Roman collar—the symbol of a Catholic priest—adorning his neck. I don't know if it was fate or a chance encounter, but it was Father Byrnes, one of my professors from Sophia University in Japan. I was so surprised to see him in Hilo.

He was on sabbatical leave from Sophia and had been a guest of the Saint Joseph Church in Hilo for several months. I was very disappointed to learn that he would be leaving Hilo just a few days later, but I was able to make a luncheon appointment with him.

We met at the church the next day and walked a few blocks down to Hilo Drug Store, where the dining area had booths for privacy. We sat down, and I apologized to him first thing.

"I apologize for the impertinent remarks I made in my essay, 'Jesuits are Diabolical,'" I told him, "and for the after-school dialogue about it, too." My essay had expressed my opinion of the equivocal nature of those who preach the church's teachings—specifically, priests throughout the ages who commit atrocities on the one hand while preaching the gospel of love and decency on the other.

Father Byrnes smiled and accepted my apology.

"Humans are fallible," he said, "but they seek solace in that fallibility by turning to religion."

The relationship between a human and the spiritual being, he said, was private and personal. He told me that as a member of the Order of Society of Jesus, he strived to attain that relationship by seeking knowledge and understanding throughout his life to be one with the Supreme Being.

I told him about the problems I was experiencing—from the rise and fall of my business venture in Tokyo, to returning to Hawai'i with a wife and son to look after, dejected, though with a glimmer of hope.

Father Byrnes smiled when he talked, but this time there was an unusual look of seriousness on his face as he told me that human beings are essentially social beings. He said that within a community, humans need to help each other in order to survive.

"Renew your old acquaintances, make new friends, and ask for help," he advised. "And when you receive that help, always return the favor and work for the common good, and you'll be accepted into the community."

He added that during his several months in Hilo he had realized that the town was full of beautiful people and multiethnic groups living together harmoniously. He was making a very strong assumption that I would succeed.

For his final words of encouragement, he said he was confident I would find a lasting career that provided spiritual comfort. That statement proved to be prophetic.

My wife, Mieko, was exceedingly capable, and she taught herself to speak English, got a driver's license, and went to work as an interpreter for a tour company. She also passed the test for citizenship and became a naturalized U.S. citizen. Later she established a convenience store in Keaukaha, which catered to residents of nearby Hawaiian Home Lands, as well as visitors to the beach parks. Her contributions to our family income enabled us to remain frugally but comfortably above the poverty level and were a big help.

With our monthly income somewhat stable, we could finally afford to rent an inexpensive two-bedroom house, though we were only barely self-sufficient. We were subsisting with few amenities for material comfort and convenience, which I especially lamented for Paul and Mieko. When we moved, my sister, Kay, gave us two beds, a dining room table, and chairs, which we really appreciated. We still needed another vehicle, as well as a washing machine, refrigerator, stove, television set, and some other household furniture.

As luck would have it, an elderly man, Mr. Okamura, heard about my return to Hawai'i. I didn't know him, but he had known my deceased father, and my father had helped him in a time of need. Aware of my predicament in starting a new life, Mr. Okamura offered to sell me his fairly new 1968 Nissan pickup truck, which had fewer than 1,000 miles on it, for a heavily discounted price. The truck had a manual, stick shift gear requiring a foot clutch, and it was difficult for him to handle in his old age. He preferred a vehicle with an automatic transmission.

He offered it to me for only $1,500 cash. He said he'd like to give it to me free, as he had enough to live on from his pension and Social Security benefits, but that he had a specific need for the $1,500.

It was a great deal and I urgently needed to find $1500. Frantically, I searched the telephone directory for the familiar names of my boyhood friends in hopes of "renewing old acquaintances," as Father Byrnes had suggested. I found many casual acquaintances, but it was disheartening to learn that most of my school friends had moved away from the Islands. The landmarks in Hilo were familiar, but it was a new generation of people that lived there.

> Chabo went on to eventually retire as county fire chief in 1984, and to this day he and his other retired friends frequently meet at the McDonalds at Pu'ainako for breakfast. I occasionally stop by to chat with them. We usually talk about our country's current political situation, especially during election years, and sometimes about the good old days when we were growing up. We repeat many of our stories over and over again, but nevertheless we always enjoy them as if we are hearing them for the first time.

I was able to find the names of only three people I once considered close friends who I felt I could unhesitatingly ask for help. They were Shozo (Chabo) Nagao, Rupert Nakagawa, and Rusty Mishima, and it turned out that they were friends, indeed, to their old friend in need.

Chabo Nagao and I practically grew up together. His father, Kanji, and my father, Morie, both immigrated from Japan in the early 1900s, while in their late teens, to work in the sugar fields. Chabo and I were classmates throughout elementary, intermediate, and high school until our junior year, when I was drafted and left school. When I met him again, he was captain of the fire station on Kawailani Street.

Although I had not seen him for twenty-three years, I still considered him a best friend. Restraining my humiliation, I humbly asked him if he would co-sign a loan so I could purchase the Nissan pickup truck. He agreed without hesitating. I purchased the truck and it immediately resolved my family's transportation problems. Mieko could now drive to her work, and I could drive to my three part-time jobs.

Rupert Nakagawa had been another close friend. When I returned to Hilo, he was working at Hilo Iron Works as a welder and fabricator of large machines for the sugar plantations. He had become a jack of all trades, having learned carpentry by helping his father, a housing contractor, build houses and had also learned to be an automotive mechanic and electrician.

He visited me after work one early evening, having learned from Chabo where I lived. He surveyed the surrounding area, looked at the water heater shed and the interior of the rented house and then left, saying he'd be back in about an hour. When he returned, he brought a used lawn mower and a used washing machine, both in good operating condition. He also brought some secondhand tools, such as a hammer and nails, wrenches of varying sizes, screwdrivers, and a saw. He went to the shed and replaced the water heater's fuse. Before he left, he handed me $700 in $20 bills, saying I could return the money when I was on my feet again. With the loan, I purchased a small refrigerator, an electric stove, a television set, and some furniture.

He and I had attended different elementary schools, but I knew him because our mothers were friends. Our encounters had been sporadic during our childhood years, yet we had developed a bond of friendship—mostly through one memorable incident that happened when we were about eight years old.

I had headed out to the Mamo Theater one morning to see *The Lone Ranger*, a serial movie that showed every Saturday morning at 10 a.m. On my way to the theater, I took a short cut across a dirt path that led to the theater, and Rupert happened to take the same route.

As we approached the rear of the theater, a huge, tall *haole* (white) man stood in front of us with a brown, sawed-off stick about two feet long in each hand. He gave each of us a stick and a dollar bill and pointed out that with that dollar we could see ten movies at ten cents, or we could buy twenty bottles of Coca Cola or Pepsi Cola at five cents each. He said we were to sacrifice one movie that day in exchange for three hours of work and $1 each.

He gave us instructions: If we saw someone approaching, we were to run the stick horizontally on the vertical corrugated metal roofing that served as the outer walls of the building, which would make a loud crackling sound.

We stayed on duty and diligent for three hours, except for a moment when I peeked through a small hole and saw the interior of the room. About twenty men and several women were gambling, some playing cards and many standing around the craps table, which had a lot of money on it.

That happened during an election year. An attorney, Martin Pence, was running for the County Attorney's prosecutorial seat on the platform of anti-gambling. He vowed to crack down on illegal gambling, which he said was causing men and women to lose their entire paychecks and neglect their responsibilities to care for their families. He had promised to prosecute promoters and operators of gambling games.

Rupert and I realized that we had taken part in an unlawful enterprise and we made a pledge of secrecy, promising we wouldn't tell anyone that we aided in the operation of a gambling game. We both kept this secret for more than half a century until Rupert passed away.

Martin Pence went on to win the election and became the new county attorney, and according to rumors, the huge haole man left the island for fear of being prosecuted.

Rusty Mishima lived at the dead-end top of Kūkūau Street, overlooking Hilo Bay. Like Chabo, he was my classmate throughout elementary, intermediate, and high school until I was drafted into the Army. Rusty seldom came down the hill to play with us, but we were good friends on school days.

All those years later, knowing about my situation, Rusty recommended I join the Lions Club and participate in community benefit projects. He thought that as a member, I would be able to meet and befriend influential members of the club. He sponsored me, and I was voted into the Waiākea Lions Club.

Club members, from the middle- and upper-income levels of the community, were presidents and managers of construction companies, and supermarket chains; small business owners; professional people, such as dentists, doctors, newspaper editors, and reporters; educators; and county and state government managerial staff. In comparison to other members, I was an underemployed newcomer and a nobody. I was quiet and unassuming, and only voted "aye" or "nay" on issues requiring a vote by members.

But once a month on Monday evenings, I diligently attended the club meetings. My biggest motivation for being there was to have a conversation over dinner with Kazuo (Kazu) Komura, whom I had befriended. He was the governor's liaison officer for the County of Hawai'i. We always sat at the same table during the meetings and talked about the social, economic, and political problems and needs of our county. It was of tremendous interest to me and a help in subsequent years.

Kazu, who was born and raised on Maui, came to Hilo and established a termite and pest control business, which he later sold in order to campaign full time for Shunichi Kimura in what was a successful bid to become mayor of Hawai'i County. Kazu worked for Mayor Kimura until Governor John Burns appointed him as his liaison officer for Hawai'i County. Kazu and I became the best of trusted friends in the following years and remained so until he passed away.

Chapter 3. Commitment to a Conviction

I was still struggling to earn a living when a job came up that was an opportunity of a lifetime. An advertisement in the local newspaper sought an "Economic Development Specialist" at the Hawai'i County Economic Opportunity Council (HCEOC), a non-profit, federally funded community action agency.

I immediately submitted my application and was called for an interview. Three individuals made up the interview committee, and the chairman of the committee asked most of the questions.

It was one particular answer I gave—on how I would assist the low-income to become economically self-sufficient—that may have convinced the committee to recommend me to the executive director of the HCEOC as one of three candidates for final consideration.

I said that most, if not all, low-income families were experiencing a way of life that was based on subsisting through government welfare benefits. I said that the only sure way for such families to attain self-sufficiency was to change their attitudes toward work, family, and community by developing and implementing job creation, job training, and placement projects so they could become contributing citizens to the community.

And most importantly, I said, we needed to strengthen the family unit by designing

> Local Community Action Agencies were formed by the Economic Opportunity Act of 1964, and they are directly regulated by the federal government. There are more than a thousand such agencies in the U.S. They aim to promote citizen participation, help low-income individuals with utility bills and home weatherization, administer Head Start preschool programs and job training, operate food pantries, and coordinate community initiatives.

programs for their children and youth to help them become adults who contribute to society, so they would not fall into poverty again.

Two days later, the HCEOC executive director interviewed me for final selection and then hired me.

Later, I learned that the chairman of the interview committee, a respected Native Hawaiian named Randy Ahuna, Sr., had seriously and resolutely vouched for me. I recalled my encounter with the elderly Japanese gentleman known as Sensei in northern Japan, and the parting promise I'd made to be kind, respectful, and helpful to the Hawaiian people. Ironically, the opposite happened: a Hawaiian helped me, a Japanese-American.

On April 1, 1971, I reported to my first day of work at the HCEOC. During the days of orientation for my new job, I diligently studied the Federal Economic Opportunity Act of 1964 and the HCEOC bylaws, particularly its mission and objectives. I came to the conclusion that I had finally found a career—and a commitment to help the disadvantaged people of the Big Island attain self-sufficiency—that was worthy of a lifetime.

Trouble at work

However, I had been on the job for only two months when HCEOC received an official notice of defunding from the Federal Regional Office due to discrepancies in fiscal and program management, with a closeout period of six months.

Mayor Kimura went to the regional Office of Economic Opportunity in San Francisco to plead with officials not to defund HCEOC. As a result, the regional office allowed HCEOC to continue, but it imposed twenty-eight special "conditions of remedial action" that needed to be fulfilled within a three-month period.

The most critical discrepancies were in the areas of fiscal and administrative management, though there were also deficiencies in program development and there was a lack of program participation by the poor. The local newspaper, the *Hilo Tribune*, had a field day investigating HCEOC and ran a series of derogatory front-page articles titled "What Went Wrong." It ran these articles daily, for more than a week, with two reporters arriving each day to search the records for clues to what went wrong.

While we were in that state of gloom and doom, the executive director resigned and took a job with the county government. The HCEOC board appointed our Head Start program director as interim executive director to carry out corrective actions, as stipulated in the special conditions. The interim executive director convened a staff meeting and announced that many of the special conditions were impossible to fulfill within three months, and he recommended the board "throw in the towel."

What? Just two months into the job and give up? My despondence turned into exasperation. I really got upset, and in front of everyone, I told him off. I was really in an uproar. I put the guy against the wall—literally. Sometimes you have to take the offensive in this world. He was a timid guy and he didn't say anything.

I told the interim director and employees that we weren't going to give up without trying; that the mayor flew to San Francisco to plead with federal officials, and we couldn't let his efforts be for nothing. I said that we could not just give up and jeopardize the jobs of more than fifty employees. I would convince the board of directors to tackle the special conditions. The employees agreed.

The next day, the board of directors agreed to take steps to try and fulfill the twenty-eight special conditions. A few days later, the interim director resigned, but then he was soon hired as director of the local United Way, which suggested he secured that job prior to resigning.

The Kona district supervisor, Michael "Mike" Needham, was appointed the new HCEOC interim director, and the next three months were hectic with remedial activities.

Regarding the fiscal problems, two federal officials came to conduct a five-day intensive workshop on fiscal management for all HCEOC managerial staff. Two months later, one official returned to monitor our accounting system and found it to be functioning properly.

As for program development, we were to write five proposals based on the needs of our low-income population—transportation, elderly services, housing, children and youth, and for the alleviation of the high cost of living. We wrote the project proposals within two months.

Of the remaining special conditions, twenty-five dealt with revisions to the bylaws, personnel and fiscal policies, and other administrative functions.

But the most critical and formidable condition was that the community organization ensure that the poor participate in community affairs affecting their lives to the maximum degree feasible.

Hawaiʻi County encompasses fifty-eight communities and townships, many of them (with the exception of Hilo) small, sugar plantation communities. The county is roughly the size of Connecticut, situated within a widely dispersed two-hundred-and-sixty-mile perimeter.

The reorganization called for dividing this county into four districts: Hilo, Kaʻū/Puna, Kona, and Hāmākua. I was placed in charge of this reorganization.

The four districts made up the four district council boards. For the community councils, a cluster of small, contiguous communities merged with a larger community.

The tasks we would perform were:

- Conducting house-to-house canvassing of the fifty-eight communities to recruit low-income members for the community councils.
- Convening three meetings for each of the designated communities within the district: one for orientation and for members to become acquainted with each other; a second for discussing community needs; and a third for electing officers to the community council, and also for electing two members to the designated district council board.

The quorum for each of the three meetings was twenty, and if there was no quorum, the meetings would be rescheduled for another day.

Two board members were elected to the HCEOC board from each of the four districts, plus an additional member was elected by the Head Start Policy Council, for a total of nine board members representing the low-income sector. The selection process for the eight board members was similar to that of a county-wide political election.

We announced the election through the media. More than two thousand registered low-income HCEOC members were notified by mail and telephone. Walk-ins were allowed if they presented proof of their low-income status, such as a copy of their previous year's tax returns, pay stubs, or proof of receiving welfare benefits.

The district council board nominated candidates, but anyone, regardless of income, could register as a candidate. We established twenty-one polling places and had ballots printed. Mayor Kimura allowed us to use twenty-one of the official ballot boxes with locks and keys that were used for public elections. We announced the election day.

The election of low-income sector board members, monitored by the federal regional representative, was successfully accomplished before the deadline. This resulted in the fulfillment of all twenty-eight special conditions imposed by the Feds.

The HCEOC was thereby composed of a tripartite, twenty-seven-member board of directors: nine elected low-income sector representatives, nine public sector representatives (county and state lawmakers), and nine private sector representatives (from civic clubs, associations, banks, the Chamber of Commerce, the Bar Association, and the university).

We were absolutely elated at our accomplishments—until we discovered that we had a problem, due to my unintentional error in allowing the staff to work beyond established work hours. The twenty-one staff members under my responsibility had accumulated a total of 3,528 overtime hours during the final twenty-eight days of working to meet the established deadline. But overtime pay was not in the budget.

At the first meeting of the new board of directors, the matter of overtime pay was brought forth for discussion. Twenty-one of my district staff members were present at the meeting and one, Barbara Dart, asked the chairperson for permission to speak. She spoke eloquently of the reason they worked the extra hours—to accomplish the tasks that would save the HCEOC—and said that our mission of helping the poor was more important than overtime pay. She informed the board that one hundred percent of the twenty-one staff members agreed to donate the overtime hours to the HCEOC.

The board members stood up and gave the twenty-one staff members a standing ovation.

In later years, I realized that process evolved into the power behind our grassroots force in the war on poverty. The district staff took ownership of the programs and activities in its district, and developed itself into a dedicated, hard-hitting, progressive team to fight poverty. The process of going through the campaigning led to our development of a grassroots power that was the strength of the organization.

Reorganization

Soon after, there was an agency staff reorganization. Most importantly, a permanent executive director's position was advertised nationwide. Along with the interim executive director, I was one of eighteen applicants for the job. I submitted my application merely to show my dedication, and at the insistence of my staff and many board members.

The interview committee recommended three names, ranked in priority order. The first was a former Peace Corps director, I was second choice, and the third choice was the present HCEOC interim director. I immediately, and voluntarily, withdrew from the competition, telling my staff I would rather stay on as program director, responsible for the operation of the four district programs. I said that, with only a few months in community organization, I lacked the experience of administering programs for the whole agency. The interim director, Mike Needham, was named executive director.

Although in the beginning I was concerned about Mike's administrative capability, he turned out to be a capable administrator, especially in fiscal and grants management.

And so the HCEOC reorganization took place. Four specialist positions were eliminated—in economic development, transportation, housing, and senior services—and two new positions were established: that of an assistant executive director and a program director. The hiring of an assistant director, however, was postponed.

The program director's position was advertised. I applied for it and was hired. I was placed in charge of overseeing the programs in the four districts, with the exception of the Head Start program.

Mike was a flexible individual, and with the exception of one disagreement, he approved all of my recommendations and allowed me to take ownership of the programs in the four districts.

Chapter 4. Politics is a Means to an End

I kept reminding myself of HCEOC's core mission: to prevent, alleviate and eliminate poverty conditions in the County of Hawai'i by mobilizing and channeling public and private resources into anti-poverty actions, in order to increase the capabilities, as well as the opportunities, of the poor in the affairs of the community that affect their lives and to educate children and youth to become responsible, contributing adults in society.

I came to realize it was necessary to mobilize support from influential people, especially elected public officials.

Hawai'i's cost of living was one of the highest in the nation, second only to Alaska's, and so early on we established a discount buying program for the elderly (those sixty-five years and older). I contacted Tom Okuyama, president of Mall Foods Supermarket in Hilo and a fellow member of the Waiākea Lions Club, and negotiated a deal to allow more than fifteen hundred elderly, low-income citizens with proper identification to receive a five percent discount at his market.

We followed that up at another supermarket with another discounted bulk-buying service for low-income elderly and the disabled residing in isolated former plantation camps that were far from supermarkets. Our bulk-buying program aide took orders during the afternoon by going house to house, as well as on the telephone, and the next morning the aide went to the supermarket, picked up the requested items and delivered them to clients' homes. Clients benefitted both from the discounted prices and by not having to travel a long distance to the market.

Youth Development Programs Impact Crime Rate

Our next undertaking, in 1972, was to establish youth development programs. These consisted of nine youth groups comprised of 1,042 high school age-youth from the communities of Keaukaha, Pepeʻekeo, Laupāhoehoe, Paʻauilo, Honokaʻa, Waimea, Kona, Nāʻālehu, and Pāhala. The groups planned and participated in projects such as a community affairs forum with the mayor and county council members; fundraising projects that sponsored *lūʻau* (Hawaiian parties); running concession booths at athletic tournaments; automotive repairs; silk-screening of t-shirts; and dances, with music provided by the group members. Representatives of the youth groups met on Friday evenings to plan projects.

One outstanding achievement by the youth development program came from the Nāʻālehu Youth Group, which was called Alakaʻi Kā Lā ʻApōpō (Leaders of Tomorrow). One Friday evening, I drove to Nāʻālehu, a plantation town sixty-five miles from Hilo, where Alakaʻi Kā Lā ʻApōpō was meeting in an open tennis court. I wondered aloud if there was a better place to hold the meetings.

"If it rains," I asked, "Where does the meeting take place?"

The districts of the Big Island. From northernmost, clockwise; North Kohala, Hāmākua, North Hilo, South Hilo, Puna, **Kaʻū**, South Kona, North Kona, and South Kohala.

They replied, "At the laundromat."

I told them that with more than forty members in the group, they could build their own youth center if they wanted. They roared in excitement and approval.

The following week, I contacted Dante Carpenter, the county councilman who represented Nāʻālehu, and asked him to inquire about the certainty that the Punaluʻu Clubhouse, formerly frequented by community and business leaders, was to be demolished. If so, we could dismantle the structure and reuse the materials to build a center in Nāʻālehu.

He liked the idea and responded within a few days that the clubhouse was definitely going to be demolished, and said he had located a county property in Nāʻālehu where we could build. He obtained county approval for the lot to be used as a youth center.

I immediately notified the district supervisor Mary Evangelista and the youth worker Anna Cariaga, and the next day we met at our district office in Pāhala. I came up with a plan that involved Job Corps trainees assisting with the dismantling of the clubhouse, and then the National Guard transporting the dismantled lumber to the area where the Youth Center would be built.

I suggested that Mary and Anna put Darlene Beck in charge of the project. She was a senior at Kaʻū High School, a gang leader and sort of a bully. Even the boys were afraid of her. She had leadership qualities, though, which could be put to good use. Mary and Anna both agreed.

Anna approached Darlene, not with an order, but by suggesting they might get help from the Job Corps and the National Guard for the project. She asked if Darlene would contact them. Darlene obliged, called right away and within three days, both organizations had approved Darlene's request.

Job Corps sent trainees to dismantle the building, and youth group members loaded the salvaged lumber into the truck. The National Guard hauled the materials to the youth center site.

> Nāʻālehu ("the volcanic ashes"), in the Kaʻū district of the Big Island, is the southernmost town in the United States, and it covers 2.2 square miles. In 2000, the town's population was 919.

Darlene learned how to mobilize resources for the benefit of the youth group from institutions she would not normally come into contact with. She also learned how to use my services to request funds needed for plumbing work, for connecting the sewer system to the cesspool, and for other center fixtures. Consequently, I applied to a private foundation for grant funds. My application was successful and HCEOC received $5,000 for the center. The Nāʻālehu Youth Center was completed.

Kaʻū didn't have anything for the kids to do. Once when we had a big gathering at the Hilo Lagoon Hotel, some of the kids from Kaʻū were riding the elevators, up and down, up and down. I asked them why and it turned out it was the first time they ever saw an elevator.

From a TGCI newsletter at the time:
I got a call from George Yokoyama, director of the Hawaii County Economic Opportunity Council. George said that he was keeping a promise he had made to Cliff Sifton before Cliff passed away.

George once told Cliff how grateful he was for that early training experience, and how instrumental it had been in shaping the work his organization did. Cliff wanted him to let me know as well.

Now in his 70s, George is thinking about retirement. He too has been sending members of his staff to TGCI workshops, so they'll be better equipped to find funding and develop programs like the ones that he has been leading for more than 30 years.

These include a mentoring program that has helped more than 4,000 Big Island high school students finish school–youngsters like Jessica Yamamoto, who at age 16 was living on her own and on the verge of dropping out. Today, thanks to that program, Jessica has a college degree and a great job–as a grants specialist for the Council.

Hearing from George, and thinking about the terrific work that he has been doing over his long career, I wondered how many other inspiring stories there are to tell. We know that many of our training program graduates are unsung heroes. Like George, these folks don't just serve their communities by winning grants. They operate programs that make a real difference in people's lives.

We want to honor the TGCI alumni by telling their stories, and by inducting them into The Grantsmanship Center Hall of Fame.

George Yokoyama will become our first official inductee.

Our kids were walking the streets, drinking beer at the beach, and hanging out at the shopping center. But the kids who joined the youth organization, they were okay. Some were different; they were really the high-risk ones. Even Kaūmana Baptist Youth Group, they saw our kids and said, "No, thank you." There are kids the system works for, and there are kids it doesn't. Their parents don't give a damn.

But we had forty-four Kaʻū kids working on the youth center, and the police reported that during the year-long construction work, Nāʻālehu's juvenile crime rate decreased by a remarkable ninety percent. We all said, "Hurray!"

With Anna's help, Darlene entered the youth center project in a national Rockefeller Foundation contest and it was awarded fourth place in the nation. Now she's Darlene Beck Vierra, a grandmother with five grandchildren, and she's still a contributing member of the Nāʻālehu community.

There were many good outcomes from the youth development program. But there were some damaging problems, too, though they were infrequent, such as substance abuse, fighting, drinking, stealing, and racial conflicts. I knew the program's well-being could be destroyed by a single negative incident, even if infrequent, that was brought up for public accounting.

Grant Writing

In 1973, I was sent to a grant-writing seminar sponsored by the Grantsmanship Center of California. I learned the fine points of grant writing and I started to apply for local foundation grants. To my surprise, all my applications, for about twenty small grants from $3,000 to $10,000, were approved.

Much later, the TGCI wrote about me coming to their grant writing classes, and nominated me as the first inductee in its TGCI Hall of Fame.

I was selected for that first-ever award from more than 115,000 graduates and felt very honored. I still consider that one of my biggest accomplishments.

Chapter 5. Politics and Race Relations

The Sprouting Buds of Politics

Kazuo Komura, Governor Burns's Hawai'i County representative, recommended to the governor that the State Commission on Children and Youth include representatives from low-income families involved in programs for high-risk and economically disadvantaged youngsters, not only retired educators and youth agency representatives for the "good kids." Just before he resigned for health reasons, Governor Burns appointed my youth program coordinator Lester Sato and me to serve as members on the Children and Youth Commission.

Kazu continued to serve as the governor's liaison officer under Interim Governor George Ariyoshi. Kazu and I met several times a week to discuss problems and needs of youth and talked for many hours, sometimes until the sun came up. Later, he became a member of the HCEOC board of directors.

Kazu knew I had organized twenty-one communities around the island, with each community overseen by capable grassroots leaders. He asked me to join him in his efforts to campaign for the 1974 governor's election. I agreed, recognizing that with support from the head of the state, advocating for programs for the poor would be tremendously enhanced.

Kazu laid out his organizational plan. He wanted the low-income sector group to be one arm of the central group, similar to the labor unions supporting Ariyoshi. This way all the apples were not in one basket, but were controlled by a central steering committee comprised of one member from each group.

> It's not known where the use of "grassroots" as a political metaphor originated, though it seemed to already be in use in the early 20th century.
>
> - In 1904, a news article about a campaign for Eli Torrance, a possible running mate for Theodore Roosevelt, quotes a Kansas political organizer as saying: "Roosevelt and Torrance clubs will be organized in every locality. We will begin at the grass roots."
>
> - In 1907, the phrase "grass roots" was used in a newspaper article about Ed Perry, vice-chairman of the Oklahoma state committee: "In regard to his political views Mr. Perry has issued the following terse platform: 'I am for a square deal, grass root representation, for keeping close to the people, against ring rule and for fair treatment.'"
>
> - Senator Albert Jeremian Beveridge of Indiana seems to have coined the phrase "grassroots and boots" in 1912, when he said, of the Progressive Party: "This party has come from the grass roots. It has grown from the soil of people's hard necessities."

Prior to my participation, however, I had to ascertain whether political campaigning was allowed. The Federal Hatch Act spelled out allowable and non-allowable activities for non-profit organizations. Kazu sought advice from Bob Oshiro, who was the veteran campaign coordinator for many governors and victorious in every campaign he conducted. Bob informed us that the Hatch Act allowed us to campaign, or even become a party or campaign chairman for a candidate, but it prohibited the use of a non-profit organization's equipment, buildings or funds, and also prohibited employees from campaigning during working hours.

On one occasion, at an all-staff meeting of my division, I told my staff that as U.S. citizens, they had the right to vote, campaign for a candidate, join a political party, and hold managerial positions within the party or within a candidate's campaign organization. I also expressed my own preference, in line with our work, for supporting candidates who care about the economically disadvantaged people of this island, the elderly and the disabled and, most importantly, the tremendous help that was rendered to the mobilization of program resources if our candidate was elected.

First Governor's Campaign—
Ariyoshi for Governor, 1974

I asked for a show of support and commitment to my proposition. All present at the meeting raised their hands in agreement. This 1974 meeting was the start of a formidable grassroots campaign force, and our first campaign was for George Ariyoshi for governor.

The group leaders from the four Hawai'i County districts were Barbara Dart of Hāmākua, Cheryl Santos of Hilo, Mary Evangelista of Puna/Ka'ū, and Ethel Spencer of Kona. Their assistants were Mildred Guerrero, Momi Mauhili, Anna Cariaga, and Lily Kong. Campaign workers were Carmen Demello, Louis Hoomanawanui Kelii, Lillian Bungula, Raymond Rominario, Margaret Hanohano, Florence Kawaihai, Helen Ortega, Joanna Gasper, Rufina De Casa, Lydia Mahi, and Ramon Pasion. These campaign workers were all my darlings, and they really worked hard.

I asked my district supervisors to select capable leaders from each community, and to request that the leaders convene community meetings, preferably during evenings or on weekends so I could attend.

Community campaign meetings were scheduled, and I attended every meeting held in all four districts. The purpose of the meetings was to mobilize supporters and voters for our candidate Ariyoshi and to educate about his stand on the welfare of all ethnic groups in Hawai'i. I asked people to contact their voting age sons and daughters, their friends and relatives, and, as a finer point of campaigning, to ask a question: "Will you vote for George Ariyoshi?" The reply would most likely be, "Yes." In the voting booth, as a natural psychological tendency, the voter would cast a vote for Ariyoshi because he or she remembered having previously said, "Yes."

I also asked my staff to list the names, addresses, and telephone numbers of all the people they contacted and to get in touch with responders to thank them for supporting Ariyoshi. Toward the end of the campaign, we had amassed more than nine thousand names of Ariyoshi supporters.

Our campaign event went on for six months. Every evening and weekends were devoted to campaign matters.

One late afternoon, I received a phone call from Kazu. He'd had a mild stroke and was calling from Hilo Hospital, where he'd been admitted for tests and observation. He said he had a predicament that only I could solve. He explained that Mrs. Jean Ariyoshi was scheduled to visit our island the following day, and she wanted to have a series of whistle-stop meetings in small communities around the island as a vanguard to her husband's upcoming election.

I told Kazu that it was too sudden—I needed time to arrange such an itinerary. But he pleaded with me, saying that only I could accomplish the task. He reminded me that I had organized twenty-one communities around the island. I gave in to his plea.

I called my district supervisors and informed them that Mrs. Ariyoshi was arriving at 4 p.m. the next day for some whistle-stop meetings. I advised them that the meetings should be very short, not more than ten minutes each. That evening, supervisors, with help from volunteers, contacted and invited community people to attend the meetings.

The next day, Mrs. Ariyoshi arrived with two young ladies. The first meeting with a large attendance was held at the Pāpaʻikou Senior Center. It took about seven minutes for Mrs. Ariyoshi to shake hands with everyone. During that time, the two ladies accompanying Mrs. Ariyoshi entertained the crowd with jokes and witty remarks and people burst out in laughter.

Then Mrs. Ariyoshi started to speak in a soft voice and the crowd went silent. She said that her husband would be a candidate for governor and needed their help to get elected.

She asked, "Will you help me?"

The crowd gave a resounding, "Yes!"

Thanking everyone, she departed for her next stop. The meeting took less than ten minutes in all, from the start until her entourage departed.

After they left, we served snacks and refreshments in order to prolong the gathering so people could talk amongst themselves about what had happened and, above all, about the coming governor's election. We held a total of nineteen community meetings; fifteen of them that same day in East Hawaiʻi and four the following day in West Hawaiʻi. In only a day and a half, most communities in Hawaiʻi knew of Mrs. Jean Ariyoshi's presence in Hawaiʻi, with the exception of only Puna and Kaʻū, and those due only to time constraints.

During the campaign, Kazu warned me about vicious people who professed to be experts on campaigning and attempted to muscle in on the campaign steering committee. They extolled their accomplishments in past campaigns, he said, and bestowed credit upon themselves for electing candidates without providing any proof of their accomplishments.

And he warned about others, who called the Honolulu central campaign headquarters to complain about individuals running a losing campaign. These individuals wanted personal gains, such as a high-appointed position in state government or lucrative government contracts.

Their self-promotional tactics were comical to our steering committee. When candidate Ariyoshi came to visit our headquarters, individuals suddenly turned up that we'd never seen at headquarters before. They stepped up to the candidate, saying that they were doing this and that to get him elected.

On Election Day, the headquarters were crowded and people poured out onto the sidewalk and street, waiting for the winning candidate to be announced at about 11 p.m.

George Ariyoshi was declared the winner by three thousand, four hundred votes. He lost Oʻahu, Maui, and Kauaʻi, but the Big Island of Hawaiʻi was what made a difference.

My group of campaigners was scattered throughout the county. I called each district supervisor and as many workers as I could, thanking them for the hard campaigning they had done.

In 1975, after the meeting of the Commission on Children and Youth, Lester Sato and I visited Daniel "Dan" Akaka, former director of the State Office of Economic Opportunity, who had been unsuccessful in his bid for lieutenant governor. I apologized for not having been able to help him, as my hands had been full with the Ariyoshi campaign. He told me that he heard from Bob Oshiro, statewide campaign coordinator for Governor Ariyoshi, that our group had been an important factor contributing to Ariyoshi's victory and that the Ariyoshi campaign had a "gold mine" for winning—the grassroots amassed by the community action agency.

Every time I met Dan, I was impressed with his humility, his sincere concern for his fellow man and his great *aloha* spirit. Dan told me he was contemplating a run for the U.S. Congress in 1976, and I immediately thought about having the first Hawaiian in U.S. Congress after statehood. I was elated, and the memory of my promise to the elderly gentleman in northern Japan flashed through my mind. Without hesitating, I told Dan to count me in on his campaign for U.S. Congress.

Youth Development Program

I hired Ronald Ah Loy as a part-time youth worker for the Youth Development Program. Ron, a Hilo High School senior at the time, was a Native Hawaiian and an exceptional worker who acted as a "big brother" to youth group members. He also traveled with me to youth centers, helping me advise members on projects and activities.

For the most part, though, his efforts were geared toward helping Native Hawaiian youngsters at the Keaukaha Rap Center. I used to meet with the Keaukaha kids, some of whom were on drugs, though marijuana was expensive so they used to sniff paint instead. Some of them stole and fought, all of which put them at high risk for delinquency. We told Aunty Abbie Napeahi, who was on the Hawaiian Homes Commission, that we needed that building, which the kids named the Keaukaha Rap Center, and she was able to get it for us. With Ron's intervention the antisocial behavior decreased, and after twelve months, those youth center members were acting as responsible young adults.

I felt really good about that program. It was really rough back then, but the kids we had in our program grew up to be law-abiding citizens—except for two who went to jail, but afterward they came back and worked for the agency. We took a chance on them after jail, and they were loyal workers. It made a big difference.

I'd been one of those bad kids, you know. My mother didn't understand me; my father didn't understand me. They treated me like a young child when I was a young adult. I could relate to those kids. It was the Army that changed me. That's where I learned subordinate-superior relationships. I learned there's a time to obey.

After high school, some of the kids in our race relations program went on to higher education, some entered the U.S. Armed Forces, and others found employment with the county government as police officers and firefighters. Still others found employment with other public departments, such as the Department of Parks and Recreation, Public Works, Mass Transit Agency, or in private businesses.

After Ron graduated from high school, he entered the University of Hawaiʻi's School of Medicine. A few years later, he came to my home one day to tell me he had graduated and was on his way to Arizona to fulfill his internship. I was elated, but, even more, I was grateful that he remembered me. One Thanksgiving Day, he appeared at my office and announced he was a full-fledged physician. I was so proud of him. They were having a Thanksgiving Day luncheon outside in the Panaʻewa farm lots and he brought me over there. Wow, I thought, he still remembers me.

To this day he still calls me. He's a grandpa now. He always tells me, "Don't smoke. Stop smoking."

I say, "That's my medication. I'm eighty-seven, going to be eighty-eight and I've been smoking since I was thirteen. Seventy-four years! How come?" I ask him.

He says, "Hey, you got good genes, that's why."

Race Relations Project

In the spring of 1975, we applied for a race relations project under the Emergency School Aid Act (ESAA) program. The federal Department of Education informed us that although our grant application received a high score, our Hawaiʻi State Desegregation Plan was rejected. I called Kazu, who referred me to State Representative Yoshito Takamine, who was also director of the Hawaiʻi Division of Local 142 of the International Longshoreman Workers Union (ILWU). Kazu knew that Yoshito was a very good friend of U.S. Congresswoman Patsy Mink. Upon meeting Yoshito at his office, I pleaded with him to have Patsy Mink intervene on our behalf. Yoshito immediately called Congresswoman Mink so I could speak to her. I explained to her that because the State Desegregation Plan was rejected, our grant application, along with the state's grant application, would not qualify for funding.

Patsy Mink made sure that Hawaiʻi's Desegregation Plan would be accepted by returning to Hawaiʻi with several ESAA program staff to help rewrite the plan. The revised plan was accepted and our grant application was finally funded. As a result, the ESAA grant application submitted by the State Department of Education was also funded.

It was awarded for a twelve-month period, and it was my first federal grant. We subsequently received six more twelve-month grants, until ESAA program funding was discontinued in 1982.

Our race relations program allowed us to completely change our youth development program. Initially, we served four high schools: Hilo, Laupāhoehoe, Honokaʻa, and Konawaena High Schools. We disbanded our nine youth groups and concentrated on working with high school principals and counselors so at-risk students would receive their high school diplomas. We terminated our agreement to recruit students for Job Corps enrollment after learning that some counselors were too eager to send at-risk students to the Job Corps. We initiated a one-on-one program to allow for more individualized attention for students and parents, with the aim of the student graduating from high school, and to strengthen the family unit with emphasis on developing a strong relationship with the high school.

At the onset, we convened a meeting with school counselors and our staff, the community counselors. The school counselors objected to our using the word "counselor," so we renamed our staff "community facilitators."

In those days there was a really big problem with racial tension, especially at Hilo High School. We knew we wanted to do something to bring the kids together so they got to know each other—just like Hanohano, who used to talk bad about Japanese but then fell in love with a Japanese girl and married her. We just wanted these kids to get to know kids of other races.

We started by convening meetings between youth from two ethnic groups: Hawaiians from Keaukaha and Filipinos from Pepeʻekeo. Members discussed the similarities and differences of their culture and its food, music, and customs, while keeping in mind that they were all Americans.

Then we added some Portuguese people from Honokaʻa, followed by Japanese, Korean, Chinese, Puerto Ricans, and those of other minority groups, and continued teaching that although we had differences in our cultural heritages, we were all American citizens and could all get along by understanding and appreciating the diversity of our cultures. We emphasized that each ethnic group contributed a part of its ways to a pan-Hawaiian culture we affectionately call the "local culture."

It was an effective program and it made a difference in the youths' lives. Through ongoing group sessions, and sharing with each other what they liked and disliked about each other, they developed more understanding. The ethnic group members became more tolerant of other ethnic groups and, consequently, violence among the groups subsided.

Chapter 6. Trouble at Hilo High

Hilo High was Hilo's only public high school in 1975 and had nearly 1,800 students. We assigned it four community facilitators, while we assigned each of the remaining schools one.

It was not only the island's largest high school, but it also had the biggest problems. Antisocial behavior, such as drinking, racial tension, fighting, and truancy, was rampant. One group of youngsters called themselves the Primo Gang, a name adopted from Primo Beer, a popular beer at that time. Articles on problems at Hilo High frequently appeared in the local newspaper.

I was curious about the home life of the school's high-risk students—particularly about the students' behavior at home and their relationships with their parents. I wondered about the Parent Teacher Student Association (PTSA). What role did it play in bettering the school so students could learn in a safe and harmonious school environment?

My curiosity compelled me to attend the next PTSA meeting held in the Hilo High cafeteria. Only five other people attended. Two were teachers, whom I recognized, and three were parents I didn't know. When the meeting was called to order, first up was a discussion about an upcoming PTSA conference in Los Angeles and who should attend from Hilo High. Names were suggested. The parent-members looked at me, and one asked whether I was a member. I stood up and explained I was just observing, but that I didn't belong there. I excused myself and left.

Two days later, I made an appointment with Principal Richard Matsunaga, whom I had known since I taught Japanese at the school in 1970. Since his school was under scrutiny, he was open to suggestions. I recommended we establish mini-PTAs in the communities served by

Hilo High for high-risk students and their parents, that our community facilitators be assigned to twenty-five "cream of the crop" high-risk students as regular clients, and that our community facilitators be in touch with the parents of those students.

He liked the idea, and we started the mini-PTA meetings, scheduling them during the evenings. Principal Matsunaga, Vice Principal Kiyo Hamakawa, and counselors Herb Zane and Al Manliguis attended as well. High-risk students and their parents packed the meeting room. Principal Matsunaga spoke of the problems in the school and about truancy, saying that more than a hundred students did not come to school each day. Some who did show up just roamed the school campus, without attending classes. He spoke about ethnic in-grouping and out-grouping, which was causing racial tensions and fighting.

The parents listened and spoke up. Many said that they didn't know what was going on at the school. One brave student said that some teachers "turned him off," and so his grades were Cs and Ds. Principal Matsunaga said that he would change the student's teachers for him. He did, and after that the student received As and Bs.

Perhaps the most critical point the principal expounded upon was that high school students have reached the stage of young adulthood, and therefore parents needed to change their attitude and treat them as such. They were no longer the babies of yesteryear. The students, likewise, must transition their thoughts and deeds from those of a child to those of an adult with the ability to think for him or herself.

As a result of the ongoing mini-PTA meetings, problems at Hilo High decreased to a manageable degree. Principal Matsunaga, Vice Principal Hamakawa, and counselors Al Manliguis and Herb Zane were true educators—they attended every mini-PTA meeting, whether scheduled for an evening or a weekend. Perhaps the reason the mini-PTAs flourished was because parents got a better understanding of education being a total community effort and their role as one of the critical cogs in their sons' and daughters' education.

I regretted that when Principal Matsunaga retired the new regime discontinued the mini-PTA meetings in order to adhere to a collective bargaining agreement stating that regular, unpaid, off-campus activities by union members were not allowed. Without school officials attending, the meetings no longer had substance.

But our four community facilitators continued to serve twenty-five high-risk clients and their parents for a total caseload of one hundred. In addition, they tracked down off-campus "no shows," who on some days numbered more than a hundred, and delivered them to their classrooms.

Locus of Control

I was sent to an orientation workshop for the Emergency School Aid Act (ESAA) program grantees at the East-West Center in San Francisco. It covered grant management, program monitoring and evaluation, and reporting procedures.

One hour before the workshop's conclusion, Dr. James Vasquez made a thirty-minute presentation on "Locus of Control."

He talked about how to foster internality in an external child and the importance of developing the concepts of "how to learn" and "how to become independent thinkers" internally in the child. Although it was a short presentation, I was deeply impressed and it gave me the impetus to develop a program for underachieving elementary school students.

The final item at the workshop was an announcement that the U.S. Department of Education had issued a request for proposals for a bilingual/bicultural program for the 1976–1977 school year. On my return to Hilo, I carefully reviewed my hastily written notes on Dr. Vasquez's presentation, "Locus of Control," especially as they pertained to fostering internality and nurturing the development of independent thinking and learning in underachieving children.

Locus of Control is a concept in personality psychology that refers to the extent to which individuals believe that they control events that affect them. Julian B. Rotter is associated with early understanding of the concept, in 1954. A person's "locus" (Latin for "place" or "location") of control is understood as either internal (meaning the person believed they can control over their life) or external (meaning they believe that their life, and the decisions they make, are controlled by environmental factors they cannot influence, or else by chance or fate).

When individuals with a high internal locus of control receive test results, for example, they tend to praise or blame themselves and their abilities. People with an external locus of control, on the other hand, tend to praise or blame one or more external factors for their test results, such as the teacher or the test itself.

I did a cursory study of why Asian students, primarily of Chinese, Japanese, and Korean backgrounds, excelled in public schools, notwithstanding the fact that they were from low-income, immigrant, non-English-speaking, plantation field hand families, and many of their parents were illiterate in their own language.

I came to understand that the core reason for these children excelling in schoolwork was encouragement. The students' backs were against the wall, so to speak, without any hands-on help from parents. But even with only the parents' encouragement to study hard, their children invariably became independent learners the hard way. This proved that the most effective way for children to achieve in schoolwork is through parental encouragement, with parental love and a strong family unit. All in all, Dr. Vasquez presented a refreshing new dimension to learning. I started to outline a grant proposal, due in early 1976, as time permitted.

Chapter 7. Daniel Akaka for Congress, 1976

At the same time, our campaigning for Daniel Akaka for U.S. Congress was gearing up. In late 1975, Dan appointed me to head his campaign for the Island of Hawai'i. The campaign's central committee convened a meeting and strategy workshop on O'ahu, which I attended, and I noticed that most of the campaign's leadership was comprised of State Department of Education employees who were friends of Dan's, as he was also an educator at the time.

I was a bit concerned that the central committee lacked grassroots-type people. They were mostly talkers, with few doers. I was told that Akaka lacked campaign funds as compared to his opponent, the formidable State Senator Joe Kuroda, and therefore each island should raise its own funds.

During this period, I found a friend and a partner, Chuck Freedman, a recently hired assistant director to the HCEOC executive director. His administrative duties included overseeing all correspondence as well as federal, state and county rules and regulations pertaining to our non-profit organization, and he also acted as a planner for our agency. He had a degree in journalism, as well, and had a lot more to offer than what his job position called for.

He was a former Peace Corps volunteer who had served on the Micronesian island of Palau, married a Palau native, and returned to Hawai'i. He was about five feet, six inches tall and slim, and when I first met him he was pale, with a drooping, hippie-type mustache and long hair. After a while, he shaved off his mustache, trimmed his hair, and turned into a clean-cut, white-collar worker.

Unlike some recent arrivals to Hawai'i, he assimilated into the local culture very easily. He made many local friends among different ethnic groups. He became one of us.

I told Chuck that I had been appointed to chair Akaka's campaign for Hawai'i County and asked for his help. He agreed without hesitation. His wit and persuasion, and his talent for expository writing, were of tremendous help to the campaign.

Akaka was unknown then to the people of Hawai'i county, with the exception of a few Department of Education staff members. However, Dan's older brother, Reverend Abraham Akaka of Kawaiaha'o Church, was well known throughout the state, so I took the liberty of introducing Dan Akaka to people as the brother of Abraham.

With only a few dollars trickling in from small donations, the Akaka campaign was unable to pay for advertisements and we desperately needed to place political ads in the local newspaper, as our opponent was doing.

It was Chuck Freedman's ingenuity that saved us. He wrote a press release and sent it to the *Hawaii Tribune-Herald*. Much to our surprise and elation, the article appeared in the paper. Thereafter, once a week he wrote a press release on a subject of public interest, such as, "Akaka proposes to make Hilo a college town to create new, clean jobs." That appealed to University faculty members, students, and education-minded people of Hawai'i County. Other releases were on pocketbook issues, such as the high cost of living that directly affected ordinary people. For a while, the press releases ran routinely—it was free publicity. After a while, however, the local paper stopped printing our press releases, probably because of demand for equal space and time by the opponent. However, one critical objective had been attained: Dan Akaka's name had started becoming known to the public.

In the meantime, Akaka's campaign needed a headquarters. By chance, there was a vacant store on downtown Hilo's front street, Kamehameha Avenue, across from Mo'oheau Park. Uncle Billy Kimi, a Native Hawaiian, owned the property, and although it was not for rent, I pleaded with him for permission to rent it. When he realized it was for Dan Akaka's campaign, he not only consented, but also let us rent the empty space at a hefty discount.

Since our grassroots volunteers lived in communities outside of Hilo,

I hesitated to ask them to help in setting up the headquarters. I turned, therefore, to our Keaukaha youth group for help. They willingly agreed to help and cleaned up the headquarters, set up the furniture and painted the headquarters' signs. The youngsters were in their younger teens, except for one who was eighteen and old enough to vote. Soon thereafter, their parents came to help and became campaign workers for Akaka. With the exception of two Filipinos and one Japanese, they were all Hawaiian.

Every day after work, Kazu, the governor's representative, came to the headquarters to discuss campaign strategies with me. He advised me to solidify the strong precincts and neutralize the weak ones. There was only one strong precinct—Keaukaha, which was a Hawaiian Homelands subdivision. The weak precinct was Pāpaʻikou, where our opponent, State Senator Joe Kuroda, had once lived and taught at Kalanianaʻole Elementary and Intermediate Schools.

To neutralize Pāpaʻikou, I asked two leaders of the Pāpaʻikou Senior Center, Mr. Inouye and Mr. Kobayashi, to allow Dan Akaka to speak to the members of the senior center, which had more than 250 members.

Dan and I went to the center late one afternoon.

> Daniel Kahikina Akaka was born in Honolulu in 1924 to Annie Kahoa Akaka and Kahikina Akaka. His paternal grandfather was born in China, and his other three grandparents were of Hawaiian ancestry. During World War II, he served in the U.S. Army Corps of Engineers, working as a welder and mechanic. After the war, he earned a bachelor's of education degree (1952) and then a master's of education (1966), both from the University of Hawaiʻi. He worked as a high school teacher in Honolulu and then as a vice principal and then principal. In 1969, he was hired by the Department of Health, Education and Welfare. He later worked in other government positions, including as director of the Hawaii Office of Economic Opportunity, human resources assistant for state Governor George Ariyoshi and director of the Progressive Neighborhoods Program.
>
> Akaka was first elected to the United States House of Representatives in 1976 to represent Hawaii's 2nd congressional district, comprising all of the state outside the inner ring of Honolulu. He was reelected seven times.
>
> In 1990, Governor John Waihee appointed him to the U.S. Senate after the death of Senator Spark Matsunaga and then later that year Akaka was elected to complete the remaining years of Matsunaga's unexpired term. Akaka was reelected in 1994, 1996, 2006. He did not run for reelection in 2013 but attended his final Senate session on December 12, 2012.

After Dan made a short speech, he turned to me and asked me to speak. I looked around at the two hundred members present and realized that most, if not all, were Japanese. I decided to speak in Japanese to lend emphasis to my humble request for support of Dan Akaka. I spoke in a soft voice, but loud enough for all to hear.

I began my speech by pointing out the positive—that most of the members present had immigrated to Hawaiʻi as sugar plantation workers and eventually became naturalized citizens of the U.S. Their sons, daughters, and grandchildren, some of whom were now young adults, were gainfully employed and had attained economic self-sufficiency.

Hawaiʻi had been good to them. The Native Hawaiians had graciously accepted all immigrants to their land without resistance or a fight. Where else could this have happened?

I noticed some nodding their heads in agreement and quietly continuing to listen. There was one group of people, I told them, that was still living in poverty and occupying the lowest rung of the social and economic ladder—the Native Hawaiians.

We had an obligation, I implored, to lift at least one of them up to become a congressman of the United States as an example for other Hawaiians to follow. Members again nodded their agreement.

I said that for the sake of returning a lifelong obligation (*onegaeshi no tame ni*) to the Hawaiians, we should put Dan Akaka in the U.S. Congress.

"Will you help us?" I asked.

The answer was a resounding, "Yes!"

Before we departed, I stressed the importance of asking their sons and daughters, and their relatives and friends, to help in Akaka's campaign and to vote for him.

About three weeks later, Mr. Inouye called me to say that the senior center members would like to ask Mr. Akaka to come to the center again.

Dan and I went to the center at the appointed time. The seniors, who were all smiling, presented Dan with a stack of one-dollar bills. He counted 199 dollar bills, contributed by the two hundred seniors who had been present at the first meeting.

Akaka's Honolulu headquarters was in turmoil. Polling by the media and other resources indicated that Akaka was only slightly ahead on Maui and Kauaʻi and that it was a toss-up on Oʻahu. But to the dismay of

Akaka's campaign leaders, Hawai'i County was down by a hefty margin of more than thirty percentage points. Considering that O'ahu made up more than eighty percent of the state's registered voters, the neighbor islands' votes, although just a trickle of the state votes, were going to be critical for Akaka to win what looked to be a very close race.

Dinner Disaster

The leadership on O'ahu was in a panic. The statewide campaign chairman came to Hilo and told me to recruit the "old boys" from former governor John Burns' campaign and assign leadership positions. Kazu Komura, Governor Ariyoshi's representative, was present at the meeting and vehemently objected to changing the leadership. He knew from experience that the "old boys" were only armchair advisors.

The state campaign chairman returned to Honolulu, but he sent the former state superintendent of education to Hilo to persuade me to change the leadership of the Hawai'i Island campaign organization. However, Kazu came to my defense again and told the former superintendent to leave things as they were.

Dan Akaka phoned me personally to say that many self-professed leaders had called him about changing leadership of the Hawai'i Island campaign, but he wanted me to know he was sticking with me to carry on as chairman of his campaign. Dan's remarks were a tremendous relief to me.

The day before he returned to O'ahu, the former superintendent ordered me to prepare a stew-and-rice dinner for a thousand people. It was to demonstrate how I should run a campaign. He reserved the Mo'oheau Park pavilion for the following day—the campaign gathering would occur after working hours.

I went to the credit union and borrowed money to purchase the necessary ingredients for a stew-and-rice dinner for a thousand. A staff of fifteen people volunteered to prepare the dinner. Barbara Dart from Honoka'a came to supervise the dinner preparations, and they worked all night and the next day. At 4:30 p.m., the dinner was delivered to Mo'oheau Park.

The gathering, though, was a disaster. Only seven individuals showed up, all from the education department, in addition to the fifteen volunteers who had prepared the dinner. That made a total of twenty-two people, all of whom already supported Dan Akaka. The former superintendent returned to Honolulu that night and never came back to Hilo.

The stew and rice were practically intact, and we delivered it to low-income families, compliments of Dan Akaka.

Our grassroots organization from Governor Ariyoshi's campaign of two years before was still a powerful group throughout the island. I asked the grassroots leaders of the four districts to repeat the activities conducted for Ariyoshi, namely, to contact only friends and relatives and ask them for their commitment to vote for Akaka. More than three hundred volunteers tackled the task.

Meanwhile, the Hawai'i County Democratic Party organized party rallies around the island, culminating in the traditional grand rally at Mo'oheau Park in Hilo on election eve. At these party rallies, Democratic candidates for all public offices are given the opportunity to speak. At each rally, I selected a representative to speak for Dan Akaka, campaign speakers who helped the candidates garner support and votes. Most of the speakers I selected came from the grassroots.

For the Hilo rally, held at Wailoa State Park, I asked a young girl named Stephanie Terlap to speak for Akaka. She was hesitant at first, saying she couldn't speak standard English and that she would be fumbling and groping for proper English words. I told her not to mind the proper English and to just speak from her heart local style, in Pidgin.

> Stephanie Terlap went on to receive her bachelor's and master's degrees, held a position in the County Prosecutor's Office for many years, and is now retired.

As she started to speak, the chairman of the Democratic party walked straight up to me and chastised me for allowing her to speak in Pidgin, reminding me that Akaka was a candidate for a high office and therefore her speaking in Pidgin was degrading to him and to the high office he was seeking.

But then, right at that instant, there was an absolutely thunderstorm of applause and loud sounds of approval from the crowd, which obviously approved of what she said, and the disgruntled party chairman stormed away. Stephanie stole the show.

Mistakes Were Made

Another blunder occurred, and this time it was my fault.

A Japanese-American man called Masa, a state government employee, approached me and extolled his accomplishments in past political campaigns. I believed him and told him about a fundraiser I had arranged for Dan Akaka at the old Kona airport.

He volunteered to sell the tickets, all five hundred of them, insisting he would have no problem getting rid of them. He was so convincing that I consented, and he left with all 500 tickets.

Lily Kong, the Kona supervisor, and her volunteers erected a stage, and numerous entertainers came to perform. Twenty-five cases of beer went into coolers, and they prepared a stew-and-rice dinner.

But on the day of the event, only two people showed up—Dan Akaka himself and Roland Higashi, a candidate for county council.

Fortunately, I remembered there was a canoe-racing tournament being held several miles away at Kawaihae. I quickly drove Dan Akaka to the tournament site, where Captain Charles "Charlie" Rose, a Hawaiian police officer and member of the Hawaiian Civic Club, was in charge. I asked if he would introduce Dan to the large crowd. He gladly took Dan around and introduced him to each spectator. Dan shook hands with nearly a thousand spectators, and Charlie made Dan's visit to this island a worthwhile event.

As for Masa, I later learned that he was a supporter of Dan's opponent. It was a vicious ploy, one that usually I would not be able to forgive, but because we were so successful in having Dan meet so many people at the canoe tournament that day, I calmed down. I dismissed the incident as one fitting the old adage, "All's fair in the area of political battle."

Masa never showed his face again.

Election Day, 1976

As Election Day approached, lists with names of committed voters came pouring into the Hilo headquarters where volunteers manned the telephones and called those voters. They thanked the people listed and asked them to call their friends and relatives and ask them to support Dan

Akaka, as well. In all, we received more than twelve thousand names committed to voting for Dan.

It was about 10 p.m. on election night when results started coming in on television. To our dismay, Akaka was losing on Oʻahu by more than fourteen hundred votes. He held Maui and Kauaʻi by a small margin, and the votes from Hawaiʻi County were not yet tallied. But the vote tally of the other islands told us that if Akaka did not win the Big Island of Hawaiʻi, he was doomed to lose. Our headquarters was very quiet and on edge, with a feeling of predestined failure.

Akaka lost practically every precinct in the Hilo district, although not by much. The only Hilo precincts he won were Puʻueo and Keaukaha. He won heavily in Keaukaha, by nearly ninety percent.

Finally, the total vote from Hawaiʻi County was announced: Akaka won in Hilo by more than 280 votes. The roar of victory resounded, and our elation hit a high note. Akaka had won in all districts of the Big Island!

The phone started ringing. The first call was from David Harrington in our Honolulu office. He kept repeating that we, the Big Island, had won the election for Akaka.

Then Dan Akaka came on the phone himself and thanked me, saying that he had had confidence in me at all times to help him win the election.

I was elated at having helped elect the first Hawaiian since statehood to the U.S. Congress. My mind flashed back to the promise I'd made to Sensei in northern Japan—to be helpful to Hawaiians. I felt very, very good about having been helpful.

There was only one derogatory comment made about the election, and that was regarding the speech I made to the Japanese elders at the Pāpaʻikou Senior Center—the one about the obligation of Japanese people to elect a Hawaiian to the U.S. Congress. The opposition said my speech had racial overtones. To me, if it had racial overtones, it was beautifully and pleasantly racial.

That year, 1976, was a hectic year filled with feverish activity. I worked at HCEOC from 7:45 a.m. to 4:30 p.m., and then after work I switched to campaign activities, working sometimes until after midnight, including on the weekends. After the election, I felt completely relaxed and rejuvenated.

Chapter 8. Moving Forward

The politics continued the next year, as a means for influencing the end and with good results. There was a request for proposals from the U.S. Department of Education in a national competition for a bilingual/bicultural program. I told Chuck Freedman I intended to apply and asked for his help in writing the grant proposal. He agreed to write the needs assessment, while I would write the programmatic interventions. He wrote the most beautiful, comprehensive needs assessment I have ever read. It's a critical factor in a grant proposal, as project activities flow from the needs assessment.

We completed our grant application, but one hurdle still remained. We needed the State Superintendent of Education's signature but he refused to sign, even at the urging of his new U.S. Congressman Dan Akaka. The superintendent explained that his own department was also submitting a grant application, meaning we were competing for the same funds. We responded by pointing out that the objective was to bring funds to our state to serve underachieving public school students, regardless of whether the organization receiving the funds was a state or a non-profit organization. But he still refused to sign.

I was disheartened on the flight back to Hilo until I suddenly realized there was another superintendent—the district superintendent of the Hawai'i School District, Dr. Kiyoto Mizuba. The next day I went to his office and asked for his signature. He signed the form and we mailed off the grant application.

A few months later, we received a letter from the U.S. Department of Education (DOE) stating that our application received ninety-eight out of one hundred points. However, the U.S. DOE requested clarification:

the grant itself was geared for a curriculum development project, whereas our project seemed to be for an operational project.

I called our new senator, Spark Matsunaga, and explained our predicament. I told him our belief that in order to develop a curriculum in full, it must first be field tested, and then the outcome of the field test would determine the project's validity as a fully developed curriculum.

With Senator Matsunaga's intervention, the U.S. DOE accepted our application.

Another question arose from the U.S. DOE's San Francisco regional office, though. It questioned the validity of Pidgin as a foreign language, because by definition "bilingual" means two languages—in this case, as it pertained to the grant program, a foreign language and English.

The office dispatched a regional office representative to Hilo. I asked Anna Cariaga, our youth worker in Ka'ū, to select a member of our youth group and bring him or her to Hilo. The youngster and I had a conversation in Pidgin in front of the representative. Then I asked if he understood what we said.

He replied, "Not a word." We got the grant.

We were the only non-profit organization in the nation to receive one. The state DOE was unsuccessful with its grant application, but our success validated my goal of bringing funds to the state to serve public schools, regardless of whether it was by the state DOE or a non-profit organization.

Our bilingual/bicultural program was renamed the Language Arts Multicultural Program (LAMP) and it received funding for five consecutive years, until the 1981–82 school year when the U.S. DOE made non-profit organizations ineligible to apply for grants.

Ariyoshi Re-election, 1978

About the time we first received that grant, Kazu Komura phoned me from Straub Clinic on O'ahu and told me he was under observation for what doctors suspected was a brain tumor. His voice was very quiet, almost a whisper, and I realized he was very ill.

He was calling about the upcoming 1978 re-election campaign for George Ariyoshi. He earnestly implored me to help the governor be re-elected and said he needed my commitment. I made a firm promise to him that I would help and heard his faint sigh of relief. He thanked me and hung up the phone.

I strongly believe that Kazu had a premonition of dying. Shortly after our phone conversation he went into a coma, and three days later he passed away.

Kazu Komura was a man of conviction who was dedicated to the well-being of the state of Hawai'i and its people. He was also a trusted friend.

The election was less than fourteen months away, Kazu was gone and I couldn't see any evident preparation for the election. I was frustrated and informed State Representative Yoshito Takamine that we needed to start organizing for the campaign.

I told him I recommended Roland Higashi to coordinate the campaign; he was the only fully reliable individual who was committed to the Ariyoshi campaign. Roland, I explained, was a member of the Chamber of Commerce and had strong business ties. With Roland's connections, Yoshito's union ties (he was the Hawai'i district director of the ILWU), and my grassroots ties, we would be an effective team for the campaign. Yoshito agreed, and a campaign steering committee was formed.

It was a presumptuous move by me, but I felt compelled to take action, thinking of the promise and commitment I had made to Kazu.

With Roland at the helm, the campaign's organizational activities started to take shape.

Dan Akaka did not face a strong opponent, and so I asked my grassroots organization to campaign for both Akaka and Ariyoshi. We added Lawrence "Larry" Manliguis, Lester Sato, Harold "Speed" Bugado, Gilbert "Gil" Kahele, and Robert "Bob" Yanabu to our grassroots leadership team. They were a tremendous help with the grassroots leadership.

At one steering committee meeting, we discussed the results of several polls. Ariyoshi was leading slightly in East Hawai'i, due to many Japanese votes, but losing by a hefty margin in West Hawai'i, where the Japanese population was in the minority.

I volunteered to campaign in West Hawai'i and took a two-week vacation from my job. I stayed at the Kona ILWU district office, where I slept on a canvas folding cot and went without hot showers.

During the evenings, I met with the grassroots group Lily Kong assembled. I asked the group members to contact their friends and relatives and ask them for a commitment to vote for both Akaka and Ariyoshi, and to join the campaign.

Just as happened in previous elections, lists of committed names began coming in. One Japanese family, Mrs. Kiyono Kunitake, her husband and daughter, are especially memorable. They stood near the KTA supermarket in Kailua and passed out Ariyoshi brochures, and practically begged passersby to vote for Ariyoshi. They frequented restaurants and shopping centers and wherever people gathered, they pleaded in broken English for votes for Ariyoshi. Mrs. Kunitake must have influenced many non-Japanese to give their sympathetic vote.

After two weeks in Kona, I returned to Hilo and it turned out that our grassroots campaign, along with the unions and businesses, delivered.

Ariyoshi won on the Big Island—and that included a forty-eight-vote victory in Kona, his most crucial and valuable district in Hawai'i County. He went on to win the general election.

Chuck Freedman had parted ways with us to campaign for Jean King, a candidate for lieutenant governor, and she also won.

And Dan Akaka won his second term in office.

Once we knew that Ariyoshi had won, we sat back and laughed at the many gaffes and incongruous happenings of our campaign activities.

One happened when the old boys at Honolulu campaign headquarters were worried about the scarcity of Filipino support for Ariyoshi. They sent a non-Filipino cabinet official to Kona to muster support from Filipinos living in Kona. From the county Department of Research and Development, the official got a list of names and addresses of Filipinos in Kona, and he invited them to a meeting.

More than a hundred and fifty Filipinos showed up, and the official gave an eloquent speech with an Ilokano interpreter translating. He made sandwiches and refreshments available, and then flew back to Honolulu, where he reported to headquarters that his mission was accomplished.

What he didn't realize was that he had spoken to the wrong group of Filipinos.

Lily Kong, my Kona district supervisor, called me the afternoon of the meeting and complained that the official told her to prepare sandwiches and refreshments for two hundred people, and she hadn't had time to call Filipino supporters from her grassroots group. She told me the official did not understand that the Filipinos at the meeting were non-U.S. citizens and therefore not eligible voters.

In January 1979, Chuck Freedman accepted an appointed position with Lieutenant Governor Jean King, and his departure was a great loss to our agency. I kept in touch with him, though, throughout his four-year tenure in the lieutenant governor's office.

One day, with Ariyoshi's victory still fresh in our minds, I was talking with Yoshito Takamine at his ILWU office when he was interrupted by a phone call from Bob Oshiro. As it happened, Bob was calling about me. Yoshito told Bob that I happened to be with him and that Bob should talk to me directly, and he handed me the phone.

Bob thanked me for the part I played in the election, noting especially our grassroots effort that was separate from the mainstream campaigning. He said it was an ace in the hole—a hidden advantage and a gold mine. I felt good and thanked him for saying so.

Chapter 9. Community Action

I went to Washington, D.C., to attend a conference sponsored by the National Community Action Foundation (NCAF), the advocacy arm of the nation's nearly one thousand community action agencies (CAAs).

Still reeling from President Nixon's attempt to dismantle the Office of Economic Opportunity, which was thwarted by a lawsuit filed by a few brave individuals, the NCAF conference was about preserving community action agencies.

David Bradley, the executive director of NCAF, expounded on the need for bipartisan support from Democrats and Republicans in both the House and Senate, in order for CAAs to survive and also to increase funding for poverty programs.

CAA funding continued during President Carter's term of office. Under President Reagan, however, funding was entirely dismantled for each of the eight years of his presidency. David Bradley worked tirelessly to restore funding after Reagan's presidency by gaining bipartisan support of the House and Senate, and he succeeded.

It was the same scenario under the first President Bush's four-year term—zero funding for CAAs. And again, David Bradley was instrumental in restoring funding so that during President Clinton's eight years in office, CAAs again sailed through with restored funding.

With President G.W. Bush, CAAs, once again, faced zero funding. And again, David Bradley came to the rescue. With President Obama in the White House, CAAs are again being funded.

David Bradley could always count on our Hawaiian delegates to Congress to support CAAs: Representatives Patsy Mink, Dan Akaka, Ed

Case, Mazie Hirono, and Neil Abercrombie, as well as Senators Spark Matsunaga, Dan Inouye, and later, Senator Akaka.

David Bradley became the most effective advocate for passing legislation and funding on Capitol Hill, including those for poverty programs.

I met David many times and also conversed with him via telephone throughout my tenure at HCEOC. Without him, community action agencies would have been wiped out and remembered only as a once-upon-a-time thing, like President Johnson's Great Society dream.

Vote of Confidence, 1980

On December 16, 1980, the HCEOC board of directors appointed me executive director by a 27–0 vote. Despite a nationwide search that turned up other highly qualified applicants, the board gave me a strong vote of confidence.

My first item of business was to reorganize staff positions.

I appointed Larry Manliguis, our former Language Arts Multicultural Program (LAMP) manager, deputy director for community services, with a transition plan to assume the duties of executive director in my absence.

He had an unusual degree of leadership skills and was responsible for directly supervising the four district supervisors to carry out programs of transportation for the elderly, disabled, and low-income preschool children; surplus food distribution of food products provided by the U.S. Department of Agriculture; LAMP and Youth Development, later renamed High School Dropout Prevention Program (DOPP); Low Income Home Energy Assistance Program (LIHEAP); and the Community Improvement Program, with input and participation from the four district council boards as well as community representatives.

He took ownership of the program, as did the district supervisors, their staff and also district council board members and community representatives in community improvement projects affecting their lives. I groomed Larry to be my successor.

In his off-hours, Larry was an assistant coach for the Hilo High School basketball team under his brother, head coach Al Manliguis. After Al retired, Larry became head coach. Under his leadership, the Hilo High Vikings won two state championships. This feat—being victorious over much larger and stronger high school teams, including some on O'ahu—was unparalleled for Hilo High School.

Unfortunately, after just a short stay in the hospital, Larry passed away from cancer. The sudden realization that he was no longer with us made me miss him acutely—both the Larry who served the disadvantaged with compassion for nearly thirty years, and the Larry who firmly believed in always giving the disadvantaged a second chance, including those individuals returning to society from incarceration. How I missed him. He was truly a warrior in the war on poverty.

I promoted Toshie Mayasaki, our accountant, to fiscal officer. She was an exceptional accountant who prepared monthly reports and followed our agency's established fiscal procedures judiciously.

I selected Lester Seto to serve as deputy director for child development programs (Head Start and Child Care Center Programs). He was a graduate of a seminary, a theological school of Lutheran ministry. Having much compassion for the poor—that is, for low-income parents and their children—motivated Lester to increase the efficiency of the child development programs.

> Toshie Mayasaki became a highly experienced fiscal officer, and in her 27 years as fiscal officer, our annual audits revealed zero discrepancies. She also trained Renee Kusano and Leslie Padaken in fiscal procedures for government grants, and they in turn, became exceptional accountants, maintaining accurate accounting of government funds. Toshie retired in 2008.

Unfortunately for us, he left in 1982 to accept a minister's position in a Lutheran church on the U.S. mainland, but as his legacy he left a compassionate and effective program for other administrators to follow.

Aileen (Calles) Correa, a LAMP teacher, was promoted to LAMP manager. She was from the first group of LAMP teachers, who were hired in 1977, and had received her degree and a teaching certificate from the University of Hawai'i at Hilo. She epitomized the definition of a teacher for our Language Arts Multicultural Program—she grew up speaking Pidgin and only learned to speak standard English in school during her later years. She was a product of our local culture, and was of Hawaiian, Portuguese, and Okinawan background. Under her leadership, LAMP flourished. When she

> In later years, Aileen Correa went on to earn a master's degree in bilingual education.

was hired by Hilo High School, she was a great loss to our program but a tremendous asset to the school.

Charles "Charlie" Rose had recently been hired as manager for the Seasonal Farm Workers Program, and I assigned him additional duties of establishing a self-sustaining agricultural training and a food service program, both for low-income individuals on welfare. The agricultural training program produced fruits and vegetables and then sold them to the food service programs, which in turn, used them as ingredients for meals sold to the County Congregate Meals and Meals on Wheels programs and to non-profit child care centers.

He was a retired police captain, an impeccably honest person who adhered to a code of conduct becoming of an administrator. This was something he had learned from his years of experience in police work.

He left us in late 1982 to accept a position in the federal Public Defenders Office in Honolulu, but I kept in touch with him over the years.

After he left, I assigned Jane Horike, our researcher/statistician and a member of our resource mobilization team, the additional duty of overseeing the Food Service Program. I hired George Hanohano, a former youth participant in our youth development program, now an adult, as manager of our agricultural training program.

Our office manager was Connie Sahagun, and we hired Joyce Madamba as a computer operator. They were an integral component of our grant-mobilizing team, which brought in more than an estimated $70 million in funding for our programs over forty years.

> Connie Sahagun left us to work for the Child Support Enforcement Agency of the state attorney general's office. Joyce Madamba remained with us until 2011.

Chapter 10. Needing State Government Funds

It was in 1981 that we received notice from the U.S. Department of Education that grants for the bilingual/bicultural program, as well as the Emergency School Aid Act program, would no longer be available to non-profit organizations.

We started looking, therefore, to state government funds in order to continue our programs. I went to state Representative Yoshito Takamine for help, and he agreed to introduce bills for our programs. He warned me, though, that the road ahead would be bumpy and full of potholes. He said I could always count on votes for the appropriation of funds from the House Committee on Education and the Committee on Finance; and, on the Senate side, from the Committee on Education and the Committee on Ways and Means (which is the money committee). He advised me to ask each committee member for support and try to obtain at least a simple majority in order to pass bills out of the committee.

I knew the task ahead would be a tedious one. Both House and Senate committees needed to approve the bills, so I needed the support of more than thirty members in all for the bills to pass; then they would be sent to the governor for the release of funds. It was a formidable task, hampered by the fact that the Senate was controlled by a new leadership regime.

Senator John Ushijima from the island of Hawai'i was president of the Senate. Senator Stanley Hara, also from the island of Hawai'i, and their colleague, Senator Toyofuku of Kaua'i, had been toppled from their respective committee chair positions. The only person I could rely on was Senator Dante Carpenter, our island's former Hawai'i County councilman, as he was with the leadership group.

Dante introduced me to Senator Neil Abercrombie, one of the new regime's powerful leaders, who told me to come and see him if I needed help. I immediately asked him if he would talk to the new chairman of the committee on education about giving me an appointment to discuss education programs. He agreed, and we scheduled a ten-minute appointment.

The chairman was Senator Charles Campbell, a new arrival from the mainland. I surmised he would be the one to introduce our bills in the Senate because of his freshman status and also due to his need to impress upon fellow senators the importance of education programs; he was on the state Board of Education for a four-year term.

The meeting, which was to have been ten minutes, lasted nearly two hours. I explained to the senator that we needed the LAMP program for third and fourth grade underachieving students who were referred by their regular classroom teachers.

I told him about some of our public schools' problems and needs. Quoting Dr. Vasquez, I said that minority children make up the majority of our public school population, but that most of our teachers are from middle- and upper-income backgrounds and are educated in an Anglo-American teaching style that focuses on teaching methods for an average, English-proficient student. Most teachers are not adequately prepared to teach our underachieving, minority group children, I told him.

The most appropriate, effective way to raise the achievement level of underachievers in our schools, I told him, was the Locus of Control teaching method expounded by Dr. Vasquez, which develops independent thinkers and learners and which we had field-tested for five years.

I showed him the effectiveness of our LAMP program by pointing out five years of Stanford Achievement Test (SAT) results, which had been published in our local media, specifically pointing out the test scores from Ho'okena Elementary School.

Before LAMP, Ho'okena's fourth grade reading and writing SAT scores ranked worst in the state: eighty-four percent were below average, sixteen percent were average, and none were above average. Within a year of LAMP being implemented, Ho'okena had made a complete turnaround: sixteen percent were below average, seventy-eight percent were average, and six percent were actually above average.

Hoʻokena Elementary School, I pointed out, was one of the smallest in the state, and so its scores truly substantiated the effectiveness of our LAMP program. Its kindergarten through sixth grade had fewer than two hundred students, and twenty of the twenty-five fourth graders who took the SAT were served by LAMP. I told him that the other six schools we served in the previous five years showed test score gains of more than seventy-two percent.

There was, I told him, a dire need for classroom teachers that could teach both the achieving as well as the underachieving students, and I informed him that LAMP provides both in-school and after-school services. During school, our LAMP staff, under the supervision of the regular classroom teacher, assists in teaching the underachievers, thus allowing the teacher to work with all students. After school, LAMP activities are carried out in two-hour sessions.

At home, students, who come from a diversity of cultures, behave according to the cultural values of their parents, and at school they are expected to follow American behavioral values. I emphasized that this is where education can have the greatest impact on immigrants' children, as well as local Filipino, Hawaiian, Portuguese, Samoan, Micronesian, and Puerto Rican children.

Another problem is that minority parents are hesitant, because of language and social barriers, to familiarize themselves with the local school system and are therefore unaware of the problems their children face there, as well as the resources available to help.

Finally, I told the senator, there was an intense need to educate both parents and children about a culturally diverse society, as opposed to a melting pot where everyone is supposed to come out the same.

The senator listened and occasionally he asked questions. Since he was fairly new to our state, he wanted to know more about the local Pidgin and how it contributed to retarding learning. I had anticipated this question and copied the needs assessment section pertaining to Pidgin from our grant application to the U.S. Department of Education, and I presented it to him.

I added that highly educated individuals who grew up in Hawaiʻi—including elected officials, such as our congressional delegates, school principals, teachers, and university faculty members—switch to Pidgin in congenial conversation with local folks. Therefore, one of the LAMP objectives was for students to be able to switch on and off, from Pidgin to English and English to Pidgin, as the situation dictated.

He asked me a few more questions, including why LAMP served only third- and fourth-grade underachievers. I responded by saying that third and fourth graders were selected at the advice of Dr. Hitoshi Ikeda, chair of the Teacher Education Division at the University of Hawaiʻi at Hilo. Dr. Ikeda advised that first and second grade is too early to ascertain whether students would become underachievers, but that from the third and fourth grade, underachieving students were more apparent.

The senator also wanted to know about our relationship with the Hawaiʻi State Teachers Association (HSTA), the union representing teachers.

I explained that, at the beginning, HSTA officials had questioned whether LAMP was usurping the responsibilities of classroom teachers. This matter had been settled to their satisfaction, though, when we explained that our LAMP staff worked under the supervision and support of the classroom teacher and assisted in teaching underachievers in the classroom.

He then asked for a simplified explanation of LAMP activities. I went over, in sequential order, LAMP activities and how they fostered students' independent thinking and learning, incorporating critical factors as expounded by Dr. Vasquez.

- Cause and Effect Relationships: It's essential to understand cause and effect in order to attribute success or failure. Students must understand that without the cause, the action or result could not have occurred. (No effect is possible without a cause). We start with examples of cause-effect relationships to help students recognize analogous situations in all aspects of life. For example, a story of a forest fire. The teacher points to a fire and asks the student what caused it, why it happened. Once the student begins to understand the cause and effect in familiar settings, he can begin looking at human examples, such as his own behavior, to systematically identify why things happen to him—that is, the causes of success or failure.
- Success Experience and Achievement Motivation: An example— John is seen studying for a math test, and then he passes the test with high marks. A student is asked, "Why did John succeed?"

The student should understand that there is a definite correlation between trying hard and succeeding. "Try hard, may succeed. Not try hard, may not succeed." For every success achieved, the student feels good: "I did it." Success brings praise from LAMP staff, classroom teacher, parents, and peers. The student is motivated to try for more success experiences, realizing that there is a relationship between feeling good and experiencing success.

- Goal-setting: Advise students to aim high, obtain As, attain Honor Roll, receive praise, be good students, and please their parents.

At the conclusion of our meeting, I was pleased that Senator Campbell enthusiastically agreed to introduce the bill, which was the most crucial initial step for funding.

Once the bills were introduced in both the House and Senate, I frantically made appointments with elected officials to line up support for LAMP. Some questioned why a poverty program agency was involved in education. My response was so that low-income children would not fall into poverty again as adults.

Most of the elected officials did not commit to supporting our bill, saying that education was the responsibility of the schools and the Department of Education. One lawmaker, though, helped me. State Representative Joseph Souki, who was formerly the executive director of Maui Economic Opportunity (MEO) and my counterpart on Maui, helped by introducing me to Representative Carol Fukunaga and many others. He also allowed me to sleep on a couch in his office and even covered me with a blanket.

> In later years, Joseph Souki became the chair of the Finance Committee, and Speaker of the House.

On the Senate side, I needed to talk to Senator Ben Cayetano, whose support was key to the approval of the LAMP bill. I tried many times to get an appointment with him but was unable to obtain one. I didn't know what to do.

Sitting in Joe Souki's office, I happened to glance at a *Honolulu Star-Bulletin* article about Congressman Dan Akaka and, *Aha!* I found a way to meet Senator Cayetano. I called Akaka's office to request a meeting with the senator. Akaka's office obliged, and I finally met with Senator Cayetano.

I asked the senator to support our LAMP bill. I explained to him that LAMP was effective in raising the academic achievement of underachieving students. He replied that if LAMP was as good as all that, why didn't he know about it. He told me he would review the bill and make his decision as to whether he would support it or not.

At least it was not an outright, "No." Senator Cayetano was a powerful leader in the Senate's new leadership group, and it was essential to receive his approval.

Day of Reckoning

Finally, the day of decision-making had arrived. The House and Senate money committees convened a conference committee to decide on the many bills to be considered. On the House side, our bill was dead on arrival.

Dejected by the apparent defeat of our bill in spite of more than three weeks of my advocating and begging, I attended the committee hearing—where something of a miracle happened. It was 2 a.m. when Senator Neil Abercrombie, a member of the conference committee, unexpectedly stood up out of the dark and eloquently, passionately spoke on behalf of LAMP. He extolled the program's effectiveness and urged that LAMP be funded in order to demonstrate to the Department of Education that our underachieving students' needs were being fulfilled.

After hearing Senator Abercrombie, the conference committee members voted unanimously to approve the appropriation of LAMP funds.

It passed! And in spite of being a frugal leader, one with the distinction of being the only governor who would leave a hefty surplus in the state coffers, Governor Ariyoshi released the funds. It was the single most fortunate and satisfying accomplishment I had ever experienced.

LAMP went on after that to receive state funding for thirty-one consecutive years.

New Philosophy About Mobilizing Funds

After that exhausting near-failure at the state legislature, I realized that mobilizing program funds was going to require the help of lawmakers. It became clear to me that we needed to support and elect those who were not only sensitive, but also responsive, to the program needs of economically disadvantaged people. It was an incredible task, but I felt compelled to take on the challenge.

I convened a luncheon meeting with the grassroots leadership from the four districts. I rehearsed with them the salient mission of HCEOC—maximum feasible participation of the poor in community affairs that affect their lives. I added that the mobilization of program funds is the only real way of establishing lasting programs for the poor, as well as for our programs and our program staff to be continuously employed, and for HCEOC to become recognized as a permanent institution in the community.

I reminded the group of the finer points of getting votes and of successful strategies employed in past campaigns, and I recommended that we add two additional strategies. One was to solicit support from candidates for other political offices, ones who supported poverty programs—eight or nine candidates per district—with a "We help you, you help us" approach. The other was to obtain complimentary tickets to fundraising events from each candidate we supported. To the candidates, it meant they were assured of full attendance to their events by well-wishers, but to low-income residents, it meant a meal for the whole family. For large events at the Civic Center, we obtained more than one thousand tickets and for smaller ones, we averaged five hundred.

At the conclusion of the luncheon meeting, I asked, "Will you help us?"

In unison, the group replied with a resounding, "Yes!"

I asked, "Can we count on you?"

And again, there was a loud, "YES!" that culminated in an esprit de corps.

I felt extremely elated and grateful for the group's enthusiasm. Those individuals were special people—all warriors in the war on poverty who took ownership of the campaign in their assigned districts.

Chapter 11. A Hawaiian for Lieutenant Governor, 1982

In late 1981, Yoshito Takamine talked to me about Governor Ariyoshi's campaign coming up in 1982. But then the discussion changed to lieutenant governor.

Assuming Ariyoshi's victory in 1982, Yoshito said, he would need a lieutenant governor who would support him and be loyal. He said that the present lieutenant governor, Jean King, was not a team player and would be challenging Ariyoshi for the governorship.

Yoshito wanted me to support State Representative John Waihee for lieutenant governor, as he would be loyal to Governor Ariyoshi.

I did not know John Waihee. I had never talked to him, nor had I seen him around the State Capitol, but I consented—reluctantly, because my friend Chuck Freedman was a critical cog in Lieutenant Governor Jean King's administration.

Remembering Kazu Komura's warning, I told Yoshito that I would support John Waihee on the condition that our grassroots group would not be dictated upon by the central campaign group, who were generals without an army, campaigning for their own personal gains. Yoshito agreed. He, too, remembered the successful campaigns, launched with a tripartite effort of business, grassroots, and labor unions as auxiliaries to the central group.

Another reason for my support for John Waihee was because he was a Hawaiian.

Soon after, state representative Tom Okamura, a former Hilo resident and the vanguard for John Waihee, came to talk to us. About twenty people gathered at the Waiākea High School cafeteria to hear Tom talk about John

Waihee's campaign for lieutenant governor. Foremost, Tom said that Waihee needed a chairman for the Big Island and asked for recommendations.

> John David Waihee III was born May 19, 1946 in Honoka'a on the Island of Hawaii and is of native Hawaiian ancestry. He attended Hawaiian Mission Academy in Honolulu and received a bachelor of art's degrees in both business and history from Andrews University in Berrien Springs, Michigan. He earned a juris doctor degree from the then-newly established William S. Richardson School of Law at the University of Hawa'i at Mānoa in 1976. Waihee started his political career as a delegate to the 1978 Hawai'i State Constitutional Convention. He was instrumental there in the creation of the Office of Hawaiian Affairs and the adoption of the Hawaiian language as an official state language. He was in the Hawai'i State House of Representatives from 1981 to 1983. He was lieutenant governor of Hawai'i from 1982 to 1986 and governor of Hawai'i from 1986 to 1994. He is the first Native Hawaiian to be elected to the office.

I immediately stood up and recommended two co-chairs—William Bonk, a haole, and Tadao Okimoto, a Japanese, for the obvious reason that Hawaiians would already be likely to vote for Waihee, a Hawaiian. It was the haole and the Japanese votes that would be crucial to winning, as his opponent would be State Senator Dennis O'Connor, who was well-known throughout the state.

Everyone present agreed, and Bill and Tadao became campaign co-chairs. I had another reason for the recommendation. I remembered they had supported Jean King for lieutenant governor in 1978, and I felt they would be too occupied with the Waihee campaign to help Jean King in her bid for governor.

A few weeks later, Yoshito called me one afternoon, saying John Waihee was in Hilo and, on the spur of the moment, before returning to Honolulu, he wanted to meet with people. Yoshito asked if I could bring some of the grassroots people to the ILWU hall at 5 p.m. for a short meeting. It was 3:30 p.m., and I complained that it was too last-minute, but he begged me to do what I could.

I called Barbara Dart and Cheryl Santos, my Hilo and Hāmākua grassroots supervisors, and just before 5 p.m., about one hundred fifty grassroots people from Hilo and Hāmākua walked into the ILWU hall. John Waihee arrived with campaign co-chair Bill Bonk, who introduced him, and Waihee gave a short speech about why he was a candidate for lieutenant governor.

He said he was a native son of the Big Island, growing up in Haina on the outskirts of Honoka'a. After his talk, he shook hands with each individual, but he missed me, perhaps because I was at the rear of the crowd. I saw and heard him for the first time, but never got to speak with him nor meet him.

As I left the hall, I heard Waihee thanking the co-chairman for assembling so many people on such short notice. I chuckled with the satisfaction of a mission accomplished.

1982 Election

It was 1982 and the election year had arrived. We established a list of candidates to support: Spark Matsunaga for U.S. senator; Dan Akaka for Congress; Governor Ariyoshi for governor; John Waihee for lieutenant governor; and others.

Ariyoshi's campaign was in good hands, with leadership provided by business (Roland Higashi) and labor (Yoshito Takamine, ILWU, and Herbert Perreira, HGEA), and our grassroots organization was auxiliary to the central campaign. But to my dismay, I learned that Waihee's campaign co-chairman Bill Bonk was a former supporter of Tom Gill for governor, who'd run against Ariyoshi in past campaigns. Therefore, there was no concerted effort between Ariyoshi and Waihee's campaign activities.

I occasionally stopped by Waihee's campaign headquarters to speak with Lynn Kawakami, sister of State Representative Tom Okamura. She and her parents worked daily at the headquarters. I informed her of our county-wide, grassroots activities to commit votes for Waihee.

Lynn informed me that their activities were the usual: sign-waving, recruiting volunteers to put up yard signs, and canvassing from house to house, all of which I felt was routine and insufficient in gaining new commitments to vote, but just going around in circles among already-committed voters.

Since Waihee's opponent, State Senator Dennis O'Connor, was well-known while Waihee was fairly unknown, I felt we needed to do more. Of all the candidates we were supporting, I felt we needed to concentrate on Waihee's campaign. I told my grassroots leadership that.

Election Day arrived.

At about 10:30 p.m., the television stations announced that vote tallies coming in from Kauaʻi, Oʻahu, and Maui showed Ariyoshi ahead by a slim margin. For lieutenant governor, Dennis O'Connor was leading John Waihee by thousands of votes.

One TV commentator predicted that even if Waihee won the Big Island, the votes would not be enough to overtake O'Connor. On the Big Island, Waihee supporters watched the television coverage and silently hoped for a miracle.

And then the final vote count was announced. Waihee overtook O'Connor and was declared the winner.

The Big Island had won the election for John Waihee.

The general election was a pushover. Every single candidate we supported won. From that 1982 election, an even more powerful grassroots emerged.

Soon after the newly elected lawmakers were sworn in, I went to see the new lieutenant governor, John Waihee, to ask him to retain Chuck Freedman in his administration. With the defeat of Jean King for governor, Chuck had become a casualty of politics; he was unemployed.

I knew Chuck to be capable of whatever he was assigned to administer and to be a team player for whomever employed him. Getting him kept on, though, would be a rare feat. Politically appointed positions are usually bestowed as a reward on individuals who campaigned for the winning candidate.

But I had to try. I asked Walter Choy, the state director of community services, to accompany me to see Waihee.

Face to face with John Waihee, I expounded on Chuck's accomplishments when he worked for HCEOC and assured him Chuck would be loyal and a true asset.

Waihee turned to Walter and asked, "What do you think?"

Walter responded, "If I were you, I would retain him."

John Waihee said he would think about it, and our meeting ended.

A few days later, Chuck called and told me that he was being retained by John Waihee.

He became an indispensable confidant to Waihee, as well as a true friend, and he was active in the two governors' campaigns that followed. Moreover, Bob Oshiro relied on Chuck for campaign media advertisements. Chuck later, twice, drafted Governor Waihee's State of the State addresses.

Chapter 12. Lull

There was a bit of a lull in 1983 after the election, but our HCEOC activities continued without interruption, enriched by program funds from the county, state and federal governments.

I expanded our agricultural training program for low-income participants by adding fifty-eight acres of state-leased land. I hired George (Hano) Hanohano, a Hawaiian lad, to be its program manager. He was a member of our youth development and race relations programs and had frequently grumbled about Japanese people being hired for higher-paying jobs in business and in government. He had a change of heart, though, when he had an opportunity to meet with students of other ethnic groups. And after his participation in the race relations program, he befriended a petite Japanese girl and eventually married her.

Under Hano's supervision, the program flourished, particularly in terms of the welfare participants changing their attitude toward work and family, some becoming contributing citizens in the community.

Hano started bullfrog cultivation and honeybee-keeping projects. Although the projects had to be terminated due to virus, mites, and other invasive pests, participants developed positive self-images and a motivation to work, rather than to be dependent on welfare subsistence. Of the participant-trainees, thirty percent enrolled in community college to pursue technical skills, fifty percent were hired for other jobs, and twenty percent left the island to look for employment elsewhere.

Under a Republican governor, the state land lease on Komohana Street, where we had our offices and conducted ag training, had been converted from a twenty-year lease to a month-to-month one. In addition, our fifty acres was reduced to only twenty.

> Hano is one of our HCEOC success stories, and he still employs the former low-income workers in his business.
>
> He was blessed with two daughters, one of whom later graduated from the university with a master's degree, is married, and has made him a proud grandfather. His younger daughter is still in high school. His wife works for the U.S. Department of Agriculture. He became a contributing member of our community and an effective member of our grassroots campaign team, mustering up more than three thousand supporters from his large *'ohana* of more than fifteen hundred relatives.

After that, Hano was in charge of our Rainbow Falls Connection's gift products, manufacturing confectionary gift items funded by the federal government and sold throughout the state. After the grant expired, the project was transferred to Hano, thus fulfilling the objective of the grant—to create business ownership for low-income individuals.

About this time, I received a phone call from Chabo Nagao, my old friend and now the county fire chief, who helped me way back in 1969 by co-signing a loan. He informed me that Rupert Nakagawa and Nobu Iwamoto, long-time employees of Hilo Iron Works, were laid off and subsisting on unemployment benefits. But their benefits were to expire within weeks, he said, and they needed temporary jobs until they could find more permanent ones. Could I help them?

Nobu was a friend from my boyhood days, and Rupert was one of my best friends who had, along with Chabo, helped me in my time of need. I hired them both on a six-month contract.

Both were licensed welders, and I contracted them to fabricate a rock crusher and hay baler, and to do bulldozer and backhoe repair for our agricultural training program. They were highly skilled workers, who, in a short period, repaired all our equipment and even did repair work on our passenger buses.

Within six months, Nobu found a job with the state transportation department repairing bridges. Rupert, a man of many trades including carpentry, auto mechanics, welding, and heavy equipment repair, was hired permanently as an HCEOC facilities maintenance supervisor. He was well-liked by all the HCEOC employees and also helped us with political campaigns. I was glad I could repay Rupert for having helped me.

1984 Election

In 1984, without an election for governor and lieutenant governor, campaign activities were not as hectic as the previous election year's had been.

With the retirement of State Representative Yoshito Takamine, his son Dwight became the First District candidate for the House of Representatives. And Senator Dante Carpenter announced his candidacy for county mayor.

We determined which candidates we would support: Dan Akaka for Congress, Dwight Takamine for state House of Representatives, and Dante Carpenter for mayor. Dante had helped us with the construction of the Nāʻālehu Youth Center, our successful advocacy for the LAMP and dropout prevention programs, and had negotiated for us to acquire topsoil for our agriculture training program from C. Brewer and Company. We also supported all the incumbent candidates running for re-election for state and county offices.

Barbara Dart, our grassroots leader for the First Representative District, concentrated her efforts on House candidate Dwight Takamine, Dan Akaka for Congress, and Dante Carpenter for mayor. Cheryl Santos, supervisor for the Hilo district, helped her in the North Hilo communities, as her district comprised part of the First Representative District. Larry Manliguis, Harold Bugado, Robert Yanabu, Gilbert Kahele, and Joe Lucas, who had been an integral component of Akaka's campaign team, joined in to help Dante Carpenter.

All of the candidates supported by our grassroots won, Dante Carpenter by a hefty margin.

Transportation Program Funding Cut

In the spring of 1985, however, there was an unexpected and almost incomprehensible disaster. The new mayor, Dante Carpenter, eliminated county funding for our transportation program, which had been in place since the terms of Mayors Kimura and Matayoshi. This would deprive our clients-in-need of mobility and meant terminating thirty-one drivers.

I frantically attempted to call the county managing director, as was protocol, to inquire about the reason for the zero funding. Unfortunately, though I placed many calls, I was not able to reach him. His secretary always replied that he was in conference or "unavailable." Finally, I tried to contact the mayor directly, but he, too, was unavailable.

The county council announced that the final budget hearing for approval of the 1985–86 county budget would be held in Hilo, and another hearing would be held in Kona the following day.

I called a meeting with my four district supervisors and told them that we needed to advocate for the restoration of our transportation funds. We needed, I told them, to transport our clients to the budget hearings so they could testify about their need for transportation services, and we needed council members to override the mayor's veto of our transportation funds. We needed maximum client participation to demonstrate that those transportation funds were vital and a lifeline for the low-income elderly, the disabled and the low-income preschool children needing transportation to child care centers. The supervisors all agreed.

We decided that Hāmākua, Ka'ū/Puna, and Hilo districts would transport clients to attend the budget hearing in Hilo, and Kona district clients would attend the Kona hearing. We would use twenty-four buses for Hilo, four buses for Kona, as well as private automobiles, to take clients to the hearings.

On the day of the budget hearing, the county council room was packed to overflowing. The hearing started with three individuals who testified against restoring our funding. One represented the Chamber of Commerce, one was a private contractor, and then the chief of police testified.

Then came our turn. Three people testified, begging for restoration of the funds for the elderly, and then three disabled persons expounded upon the need for the wheelchair-bound. Finally, three low-income parents talked about the need to transport children to preschool child care centers.

Councilman Steve Yamashiro asked for discussion. All spoke in favor of restoring the transportation funds in full. A motion was made and seconded, and the transportation budget was approved by a 9–0 vote. It was a fitting victory for the HCEOC clients. They had helped themselves.

The next day, the local newspaper headline was about the county budget hearing. It was news that extolled the grassroots power. I received numerous calls from our clients and supporters of our programs who said that next time, they wanted to testify for the people. It seemed that especially the elderly were awakened and rejuvenated and wanted to again be active in community affairs.

In the following year's budget, the mayor again eliminated our transportation funding, and again, we mobilized our clients to storm the county council budget hearing. The council once again restored our funding in full by a 9–0 vote. It happened again in 1987, and again the funding was unanimously restored by the county council, with our clients in full attendance

Finally, in 1988, at the end of his four-year term, the mayor's budget contained our transportation funding, though at an appreciably reduced amount. That year, the council again voted 9–0 for full funding.

Chapter 13. The Advocacy and Power of the Press

In the early 1980s, Dr. Hitoshi Ikeda, chair of the Teacher Education Program of the University of Hawaiʻi at Hilo (UH Hilo) informed me that the university was abolishing the Teacher Education Program, and students would need to transfer to the Mānoa campus on Oʻahu to continue their study to become certified teachers. This despite the fact that many students were from low-income families, and the prohibitive cost of expenses they would incur if they had to go to Mānoa would mean abandoning their goal of becoming certified teachers. Moreover, according to a study by the State Department of Education, there would be a teacher shortage within four years and the DOE would be recruiting teachers from the U.S. mainland.

I told Dr. Ikeda that we could advocate for the retention of the Teacher Education Program, but he declined, saying that as chair of the program, once a decision had been made to abolish the program, he must adhere to the chain of hierarchy and abide by that decision. Therefore, I personally advocated for the retention of the Teacher Education Program at UH Hilo. I determined the participation of low-income students in this, an affair of the university that truly affected their lives, to be an important community action intervention.

We called a meeting of current and former students who had graduated from the Teacher Education Program and invited the dean, Dr. David Purcell, to attend and hear the students' needs, particularly the monetary hardships some students from low-income families would have if they had to transfer to UH Mānoa.

Aileen Correa, our LAMP manager, spoke eloquently about her involvement in the establishment of a four-year college in Hilo. She talked about the many low-income students who could not attend UH Mānoa because of a lack of funds and about being a product of UH Hilo with a degree and a certified teachers' credential. Many others spoke in favor of retaining the program. The dean must have been surprised to learn that most, if not all, of the students were from low-income families.

Dean Purcell responded by saying that the abolition of the Teacher Education Program was approved by the chancellor of UH Hilo and was already a done deal. He cited, as the reason, that enrollment in the Teacher Education Program was below the required number of students for the program.

The meeting with the dean was unfruitful. Dejected and defeated, we went home.

The next step was when President Simon of the University of Hawai'i visited Hilo. We sat in a meeting room at the Naniloa Hotel for a small community forum and discussion on the future of UH Hilo. Several people brought up the termination of the Teacher Education Program and the importance of continuing the program. President Simon "took the concern under advisement" and promised that he would look into it.

And then there was a glimmer of hope. A newspaper reporter got wind of our meeting with the dean and wrote an article that appeared in the *Honolulu Star-Bulletin*. He quoted remarks made by the UH Hilo chancellor which, I noted to my dismay, were untrue. For instance, he stated that Dr. Ikeda, the chair of the program, was disgruntled about the abolishment of the Teacher Education Program, had had secret meetings with students and community people, and that he diabolically orchestrated dissension about the termination of the program.

I was compelled to submit a refutation to the chancellor's comments. In my Letter to the Editor in response, I stated that the chancellor's comments were damnable lies and that Dr. Ikeda was not involved in convening the community meeting. I wrote that I had convened the community meeting with students, former students, and community people on my own initiative. I wrote that there had been no secret meetings and that Dr. Ikeda had not attended nor participated in conversations on the subject matter.

Two days later, I received a registered letter from the editor of the *Honolulu Star-Bulletin* asking me to sign a statement saying that I originated and signed that letter to the editor. I signed the statement and two days after that, my letter was published in the *Star-Bulletin*.

As the saying says, "What goes around, comes around." Some members of the Board of Regents of the University of Hawai'i read the article and my rebuttal. Regent Robert (Bobby) Fujimoto, who represented the Big Island, supported retaining the Teacher Education Program, and that signaled there was hope for the program to continue. The regents and President Simon deliberated and the Teachers Education Program was allowed to continue. It flourished and produced exceptional teachers for our public schools for years to come.

Chapter 14. Waihee for Governor, 1986

Also in 1985, Yoshito Takamine asked me to accompany him to meet with lieutenant governor John Waihee. He wanted to determine Waihee's intention—whether or not he would be a candidate for governor in 1986, since Governor Ariyoshi would be stepping down.

Waihee said that in spite of his one term as lieutenant governor, he would like to be a candidate for governor. However, he said, if Congressman Dan Akaka was thinking of running, he would defer to him. John Waihee was an honorable person, respecting the silent protocol of yielding to the most senior candidate.

I was chosen to ask Akaka of his intentions. It so happened that I was to attend a conference in Washington, D.C. in a few weeks, where I met with Dan Akaka. I told him that John Waihee wanted to know about his political plans, specifically regarding a run for governor. Akaka replied that he had come to like Congress and would like to continue serving the people of Hawai'i in Congress.

I informed Yoshito of Akaka's decision to remain in Congress, and Yoshito relayed the message to Waihee. Thereupon, Waihee announced his candidacy for governor. Congressman Cec Heftel also announced his candidacy. Early polls showed Heftel leading by more than thirty percentage points. Another poll had Waihee losing by thirty-six percent.

Mike Amii, a trusted assistant to Bob Oshiro, called to say that Bob wanted to talk to me about the upcoming John Waihee campaign, so I flew to Honolulu. Mike picked me up at the airport and drove me to Bob's office in Wahiawā, where he opened the door and told me to go in. I asked Mike if he would be accompanying me, but he said that Bob wanted to talk to me privately, and he closed the door behind me.

Bob greeted me with a handshake. I had talked with him by telephone on countless occasions, but this was our first face-to-face meeting. I noticed that he was of diminutive stature—about my height, five feet, two-and-a-half inches. He motioned for me to sit in a chair in front of a wall that bore a schedule-of-implementation chart.

He pointed to the chart with a stick and explained to me, step-by-step, what needed to happen to carry out the campaign. He had the plan all laid out, and it was a masterpiece. A person-to-person, grassroots campaign, he stressed, was the only sure way to win.

He believed that the usual efforts—sign-waving to strangers, house-to-house visits to strangers' homes, and media advertisements—were only superficial efforts; the core of successful campaigning should be friend-to-friend and relative-to-relative contacts that commit voters. Then, he said, we should have the committed voters contact their friends and relatives to expand on voters for Waihee. He re-emphasized that the campaign must be backed up by grassroots effort.

I told Bob that we had twenty-one Big Island communities that had been organized since 1971 and that in some areas two or more small communities were consolidated into one larger one. Bob agreed that the Big Island grassroots campaign was well-organized and in good hands. He had called me to Wahiawā so I could be apprised of his overall campaign strategy.

He knew I had done as he had outlined, he told me, and he reiterated that I had a goldmine of powerful grassroots from the first Ariyoshi campaign in 1974. This information, he recalled, had been passed on to him by Kazuo Komura, the Big Island liaison for Governor Ariyoshi.

It was an honor to be praised by Bob, because he was the guru of gubernatorial campaigns and had never had a single loss. We parted with a handshake and my promise to launch a double-effort campaign.

As we drove back to the airport, Mike told me that Bob was relying on me to deliver the Big Island for Waihee. He also told me to call him if I needed anything for my grassroots campaigners, such as T-shirts, brochures, etc.

I would, I realized, be running a separate grassroots campaign for Waihee, as an auxiliary to the Big Island's central Waihee campaign. Bill Bonk would continue to serve as Waihee's campaign coordinator, despite the fact he didn't seem to get along with Bob during past elections. In the recent past, Bill had supported Tom Gill for governor against Bob's candidates, John Burns and George Ariyoshi, in very heated elections. Both men's objectives were the same, though—to win the election for Waihee. It was in leadership style that Bill and Bob differed.

I was in the precarious position of having to maintain peace within the Waihee campaign. I suggested to Yoshito Takamine that we again form an auxiliary component to the central campaign, one with business, labor, and grassroots units, as we had for previous ones. To my dismay, Yoshito told me that his union, the ILWU, had not yet endorsed Waihee—moreover, the union was leaning towards endorsing Waihee's opponent, Cec Heftel.

In frustration, Yoshito threatened to resign from his position as director of the Hawai'i division of the ILWU Local 142. Yoshito's commitment to John Waihee was so important to him he was willing to lose his job over it. Eventually, the ILWU conceded and endorsed Waihee.

Our auxiliary group represented practically all of the private and public labor unions, the grassroots, and some people from the business sector, and it was a powerful one. We had lost some business sector support because Heftel was a businessman who owned television and radio stations. Large businesses tended to support Heftel. But most small business owners were with us.

The auxiliary leaders met twice a week at the ILWU conference room to provide manpower and support to the central group. Yoshito Takamine, Roland Higashi, and I met separately with HGEA director Herbert Perreira at his home to tie up loose campaign ends. At one meeting, I suggested a strategy for putting up yard signs: that whenever someone placed a yard sign, the resident's name, telephone numbers, and address be sent to the campaign headquarters so a worker could call and thank them, as a second contact. Whenever there was a campaign gathering coming up, we could invite them and provide complimentary tickets—a third contact. By increasing the number of contacts, they would be more likely to support and vote for our candidate.

It worked. Many residents became supporters of Waihee and volunteered their services. Roland Higashi and Stan Roehrig, along with their friends, took ownership of the yard sign activities and covered most of Hilo. Waihee signs were conspicuously displayed in many yards.

Visiting Ka'u

Bob Oshiro called and said he would like to visit the Ka'ū district and meet with Hawaiians there. I asked Mary Evangelista and Anna Cariaga, both full-blooded Hawaiians married to Filipinos, to call the resident Hawaiians of Pāhala and Nā'ālehu and invited them to a meeting with Bob.

We met at the Ka'ū High School gym, and the event was well-attended. Bob started his talk by extolling King Kamehameha, unifier of the Hawaiian kingdom. Then he talked about John Waihee as the next Hawaiian unifier of the state—the first governor of Hawaiian descent—and rallied the crowd to vote for Waihee.

Anna Cariaga was smiling when she interrupted and said, in a teasing manner, "Mr. Oshiro, when you come to Ka'ū, please don't talk nice about King Kamehameha, because he ambushed our king and killed him." Kamehameha is a highly regarded chief among Hawaiians in general, but as in any group, there are factions; he is not a favorite in Ka'ū, because he killed their beloved chief in battle. The crowd burst out in laughter, but then pledged to vote for John Waihee.

Mike Amii called the next day and told me about Bob's gaffe regarding King Kamehameha. When he got back to Honolulu, Bob had told his friends about the incident. He was a little embarrassed but had to admit his error.

A week later, Mike informed me that Bob wanted to see me again. He picked me up at the airport and drove me to Waihee's headquarters.

When I entered the front office, a man sitting behind a desk stopped me. His voice was loud and arrogant and he quickly fired questions at me in rapid succession: "What you want? What you're doing? Where you from? What's your name?"

Before I could respond, another door opened. Bob Oshiro stood there and he beckoned me to come in. The man in the front office tried to follow us, but Bob motioned for him to stay out. After we had closed the door, I told Bob I objected to the arrogant and dictatorial treatment I had received from the individual at the front desk.

The man in the front office, it turned out, was one of the "old boys" from Governor Ariyoshi's era, and he was trying to hang on to political power.

Bob took a folded piece of paper from his desk drawer and handed it to me. It was a typewritten statement declaring that Robert Oshiro had the sole authority to conduct his campaign for governor, and it was signed by John Waihee.

Serious campaign discussion followed. He said that although we were showing gains in the political polls, Waihee was still behind and we needed to double our efforts. Doubling our efforts meant increasing committed voters two-fold. If we did that, Bob was confident we would win the election.

The election was in two months and polls showed Cec Heftel leading, although his lead had narrowed from thirty percent to fifteen. We still had a long way to go to overtake him.

I called our grassroots leaders and instituted a voter commitment drive. We had committed eight thousand, the number amassed in previous campaigns, but I felt that at least another eight thousand committed votes were needed. I pleaded with the grassroots leaders to contact the already committed voters and ask each of them to commit at least one additional voter in order for Waihee to win. I thought this would not be too much of a burden.

Committed voters' names came pouring in. Many were duplicates and triplicates, but I felt that the more duplication there was, the more a voter would be convinced to vote for Waihee. As it turned out, though we requested each committed voter bring in one more committed voter, many of them turned in five or more additional commitments.

I also called Lynn Kawakami, at the Waihee campaign headquarters in Hilo. I'd asked her to contact the more than five hundred Waihee campaign workers there, ask each to commit at least twenty family members or friends, and turn in the committed voters' names at headquarters on the eve of the Democratic Grand Rally at Moʻoheau Park.

Later, when I asked Lynn for the list of committed names, she told me they'd had very disappointing results. Of the more than 500 Waihee campaign workers, only two individuals had submitted committed names. One had committed eighteen names and the other, twenty.

When I thought about it, I realized that these were people with no experience in asking even their friends and relatives, and so it was hard for them. Or maybe they simply didn't have time to ask—I could see them coming home from work, watching the evening news, having dinner, taking a bath, turning on the TV again for a favorite program and then going to bed. They did not have, or did not make, the time to call their friends and relatives. This was in stark contrast to our grassroots people, who habitually allocated time to call and commit people.

Grassroots Help

During our several months of campaigning for Waihee in 1986, many other notable individuals helped with our grassroots efforts.

We learned that Nelson Doi would speak for Cec Heftel at one of the Democratic rallies in Keaʻau. Nelson Doi—a former state senator, lieutenant governor, and third circuit judge—was an eloquent and dynamic speaker, and Waihee's steering committee hurriedly met to select someone who would be equally eloquent and as convincing. Several names came up, but they weren't a good enough match for Doi.

Brian DeLima's name popped into my head. Brian DeLima was a young attorney and fresh out of college. I heard him give a speech once and had been emotionally moved by it. I highly recommended him to the committee, emphasizing that he was a novelty and also represented the new and the young (versus the old). I assured them that Brian could be just as eloquent as Doi, and after some discussion, the committee agreed.

Doi spoke first at the Democratic rally. He spoke of Heftel's accomplishments in Congress and talked highly of his business acumen and leadership. At the end of the speech, there was fairly loud applause.

Brian DeLima spoke next. In a loud, clear voice, with emotion, he extolled the merits of the young candidate John Waihee. The crowd was silent and listened to every word he uttered. The moment his speech ended, there was thunderous applause, along with a lot of whistling and yelling. Young Brian DeLima had outdone Nelson Doi.

Brian was later elected to serve on the county council and became its chairman. He was also elected chairman of the county Democratic party. He considered running for mayor, but changed his mind to become a successful practicing attorney.

Donald Abe, a native of Pepeʻekeo, got work with HCEOC in its fiscal office. During the first Akaka campaign for Congress, Donald helped with campaign activities, including recruiting voters. I was surprised to learn that during a time when interracial marriages were frowned upon, especially by the Japanese, and despite his having a prominent uncle (Judge Kazukisa Abe had been a senator), he had Filipino, Hawaiian, and Micronesian relatives. Donald had committed all of them to vote for Dan Akaka, and later for John Waihee.

Donald returned to Hawai'i after nearly twenty years of civilian service with the U.S. government in Kwajalein. He took ownership of his daily duties in HCEOC's fiscal office and meticulously examined purchase orders, sick leave, vacation time, time sheets, temporary disability insurance, and Pension Plan disbursements, even though he was of the old guard and didn't use a computer. On many occasions, he found errors that computer operators had made in computer-generated records and reports.

James "Jimmy" Correa distinguished himself while supervisor of the County Parks and Recreation department by coaching young boys to excel in baseball. His team became the Colt League's national champion and put Hilo on the map. After he retired from Parks and Recreation, he helped us tremendously in committing votes. When he came to campaign headquarters to help, he sat next to the telephone with two workers assisting him. He called out a name and a worker searched through the telephone directory and then read out the number. Another worker dialed the number and passed the phone to Jimmy. He had helped thousands of boys, now in their young adulthood and of voting age. Now on the phone he asked them how their mother, father, brother(s), and sister(s) were doing. He told them he needed help with their votes for Akaka and Waihee. The response was always positive, perhaps because of the player-coach relationship that had developed over the years where players could not say "No" to their coach. Jimmy's daughter, Aileen, who worked for me, tallied up the number of their Big Island relatives and counted more than 650 who were of voting age. Both Jimmy and Aileen were of tremendous help in the elections of whichever candidates we were supporting.

Harry Onouye was a colleague of Steve Querobin; both were firefighters with the county fire department and members of the union. Steve was the first-ever union member to endorse Dan Akaka. With his help, Akaka received the endorsement of the Firefighters' Union. Harry endorsed Dan Akaka for Congress and Waihee for governor. We relied on him for manpower at fundraising events, and his assistance extended to other candidates we supported as well. To this day, Harry actively supports our candidates.

Along with these special and sometimes unexpected people who showed up with their wholehearted talents and support, I have cherished the power of our grassroots organization from 1974 to the present. It was made up of so many people and leaders that I value.

The Next Generation

Bob Oshiro wrote down two names on a card—Gerald DeMello and Alfred "Butch" Castro—and told me that these two, a generation behind us, would be tomorrow's leaders. I asked our auxiliary group to include Gerald and Butch on our team. I found both of them to be energetic, and they tackled assigned tasks with enthusiasm. They became the liaison between our central and auxiliary groups.

Gerald was also elected chairman of the county Democratic party, at a time when party membership was beginning to dwindle. To increase membership, he established a membership recruitment drive at a county Democratic party convention by appointing twenty members as deputy party chairs. He hoped the deputies would recruit new and young members. Twenty-four "old boys" and "old girls" walked out of the convention in protest. It was apparent that they didn't want new members, but wanted to maintain the status quo.

Gerald was thinking ahead, trying to expand the party's numbers and strengthen it using new ideas. He wanted to create a party that represented all segments of the community with new, fresh, and meaningful goals.

Butch became a reliable campaigner. He took charge of placing campaign banners and yard signs in conspicuous and visible locations and always covered the whole of Hilo. He handled numerous tasks that the campaign needed done.

Also, Ben Cayetano needed to solidify Filipino support and I was asked to help with his campaign for lieutenant governor by participating in all of the Filipino gatherings at the ILWU Hall. I agreed to help because Ben supported our LAMP program. We brought more than two hundred Filipinos, all American citizens (many of them naturalized) from Puna, Keaʻau, Hilo, Pāpaʻikou, and Pepeʻekeo, to a Cayetano gathering at the ILWU. It was a thank you for his supporting LAMP.

Primary Day, 1986

When the primary Election Day arrived, we were all glued to the TV and we were thrilled to see that Waihee was victorious. We had overtaken Heftel.

Our grassroots had amassed more than sixteen thousand committed voters for Waihee. I estimated that of the sixteen thousand commitments, twenty-five percent, or four thousand, failed to vote and fifteen percent actually voted for the opposition.

But sixty percent, or nine thousand six hundred, voted for Waihee.

I went to Waihee headquarters in Honolulu at Bob Oshiro's request, where Bob acknowledged that I had come from behind with a very heated campaign victory. However, he said, we could not take anything for granted in the general election because the opposition, Republican "Andy" D.G. Anderson, was a former state senator and a businessman who was well-known throughout the state. Furthermore, former Heftel supporters might grudgingly switch to supporting the Republicans, since many were business people just like the candidate.

Larry Manliguis (left), John Waihee (right)

He reminded me to be vigilant and cited what happened to the heavily favored Cec Heftel—he went down in defeat at the critical stage of the campaign. He pointed out that the same thing could happen to Waihee in the general election.

However, it was needless. Waihee breezed to victory over Anderson in the general election and became the first Hawaiian governor of the state of Hawai'i. I felt gratified that I was able to fulfill part of my promise to the elderly sensei of yesteryear and be of help to Hawaiians.

Ben Cayetano was elected the state's first Filipino lieutenant governor.

As Bob Oshiro predicted, both Butch and Gerald became leaders in government as well as in the county Democratic party. Gerald was appointed Governor Waihee's Big Island liaison officer, and Butch went to work for the State Department of Human Services. When Gerald took a position as director of Community Relations at the University of Hawai'i at Hilo, Butch became the governor's liaison officer.

Mobilization of Resources, 1986

When Governor Waihee took office in 1986, the state was in a fiscally sound condition and had an appreciable surplus. This was because of outgoing Governor Ariyoshi's frugality and expert financial management; he was the only governor to end his term of office with a large surplus of funds in the coffers. Waihee, on the other hand, was known for his generosity and did not end his term with a surplus.

Although we successfully obtained federal grants through national competitions, they were sporadic; not only because they were scarce, but also because there was intense competition. For example, in some cases, only about ten percent of some two hundred fifty to three hundred applications received grants.

It was time—and an opportune moment—to advocate for some state program funds. We conducted a community needs assessment, which revealed that Hawai'i County was cursed with several dire problems. I say "cursed" because the calamities were never-ending. In fact, as the years went by they were getting worse, becoming more and more severe.

An assessment in 1986 revealed that Hawai'i County had the highest unemployment rate in the state, at 7.4 percent. In proportion to its population, our county had the state's highest number of welfare and food stamp recipients, nearly double that of the other three counties. And based on data from the State Department of Human Services, twenty-two percent of its population lived in poverty. This was compounded by data indicating that Hawai'i County's cost of living was the highest in the state and also had the lowest per capita income.

> And in fact it only got worse; by 2010, unemployment had climbed to 9.3 percent.

A Mental Health Association survey done at the time indicated that twenty-one percent of students in Grades 6 to 12 needed substance abuse treatment. Thirty-one percent of all domestic abuse protective orders in the state were filed in Hawai'i County, the highest rate of family abuse in the islands.

Based on this information, we submitted seven grant applications to the state legislature. They were for programs in substance abuse prevention, renewable energy, language arts multicultural program (LAMP), dropout prevention, agricultural training, food services, and supplemental transportation services. The legislature appropriated the funds for all seven grant requests, and the governor released the funds.

We had good friends who believed in and supported programs for the economically disadvantaged, especially Joseph Souki, Speaker of the House of Representatives, who was a longtime friend of mine from Maui and, as I mentioned before, my former counterpart at the Maui Economic Opportunity; also Dwight Takamine, chairman of the House Committee on Labor and Industrial Relations, and Calvin Say, chairman of the House Committee on Finance. Senators Norman Mizoguchi and Mamoru Yamasaki helped our grant applications to be appropriated on the Senate side.

Chapter 15. Significant People

In the early 1990s, we hired Ruth Walker, a retired public elementary school principal, to manage our Language Arts Multicultural Program (LAMP). She replaced Marilyn Hirata, a very capable person who left to take a job teaching elementary school in the public school system. This was one of our aims—for our teachers to be hired by public schools, so they would receive an appreciable raise in salary and other DOE benefits. Many of our LAMP teachers became classroom teachers, hired after principals interviewed them among other top candidates. Our teachers were well-prepared and had the right answers to the principals' questions.

Ruth was a seasoned administrator, groomed over a lifetime of working in education. Under her leadership, reports from schools that operated LAMP were submitted on time, the staff became more diligent, and LAMP class activities were conducted according to schedule. Ruth was also an avid campaigner and joined our grassroots efforts.

After she left our agency, Courtney Hamakawa, a LAMP teacher at Kapiʻolani Elementary School, was promoted to LAMP program manager. Under his management, underachieving students continued to improve, many of them even attaining honor roll status. Honor roll recognition was discontinued, unfortunately, after the 2004–2005 school year. This was regrettable because one of our students' highest goals was always to get on the Department of Education's honor roll.

Mary Finley was in charge of our low-income housing preservation program, and she was a person I could always rely on to carry projects to a successful conclusion. That program aimed to repair and prolong the use of a house for approximately twenty years, therefore keeping the house available for low-income residents. She was also in charge of a home energy assistance project, which helped low-income households save electricity by installing solar water heaters. After that, she distinguished herself by tackling our self-help housing projects at Miloli'i fishing village. And then the twenty-eight new homes we got built on Hawaiian Home Lands in Keaukaha and Pana'ewa.

In April 1988, we received $500,000 from the state to administer a self-help housing program for twenty-two low-income families from Miloli'i. We received three additional contracts for self-help housing projects, as well: $47,000 for second-phase construction of additional homes at Miloli'i; $750,000 for twenty-two homes from the Department of Hawaiian Home Lands in May 1993; and $350,000 for eight homes completed in 1996.

The $18,000 to $25,000 two- and three-bedroom, two-story homes in Miloli'i became showcases for affordable housing for the low-income, with fixed monthly mortgages of about $140. Mary Finley managed that project.

Mary was an effective and intelligent individual, and I sent her to the Grantsmanship Center to take a course in grant writing. She was also an effective campaigner and helped our grassroots leadership.

Max Goldberger

Dr. Max Goldberger, a physicist who specialized in clean energy technology, was a comrade-in-arms for twenty-four years, from 1988 until his death in 2012. He helped fight the war on poverty and served the Big Island's disadvantaged people well.

Dr. Max was an amazing person. He was well-known within the scientific community and very accomplished, holding patents in hydrazine technology, fuel cells, torpedo propulsion, and remote control. He served as an adviser to many governments, such as those of the Philippines, Israel, Taiwan, Thailand, Jordan, Uganda, Zambia, Somalia, and Switzerland.

He was born in what is now Romania and spent three-and-a-half years in a Nazi concentration camp but managed to survive the Holocaust—though his siblings and other relatives died in the gas chamber—by using his knowledge of seven languages and his mastery of technology.

He served as the HCEOC's director of science and technology, and added a new dimension of job training to our energy and technology projects. Trainees gained technical skills by participating in projects such as providing electricity, using photovoltaic cells, to the new homes in Miloliʻi; that was in the 1980s, when photovoltaic was a novelty. Trainees learned about Fresnel lens tooling, how to eradicate papaya fruit flies using a pressurized steam in a retort chamber, how to desalinate sea water for drinking, and how to generate electricity from thermoelectric modules and other energy devices.

One of his notable contributions to the state of Hawaiʻi was his work on the 1990 World Hydrogen Energy Conference in Honolulu, which was sponsored by the University of Hawaiʻi. The university tried to obtain a hydrogen fuel-powered automobile for the conference from Mercedes-Benz in Stuttgart, Germany, but was unsuccessful and asked Dr. Max for assistance. He got in touch with his colleague Dr. Gerd Sandstede, a well-known scientist who had received West Germany's highest award in science, and Mercedes-Benz sent a hydrogen-powered research automobile to Hilo free of charge. This epitomized the essence of the hydrogen conference.

Dr. Max was also a member of our political grassroots campaigning group. He usually helped by contacting Jewish community residents to support our candidates. In 2008, when Dwight Takamine was running for the Senate, our poll indicated that the Waimea district was showing signs of weakness for Dwight, due to an affluent white population that tended to vote Republican. Dr. Max contacted fellow scientist Dr. Earl Bakken, and implored him to assist in supporting Dwight.

Dr. Bakken was a highly respected community member who invented the pacemaker, founded North Hawaiʻi Community Hospital, and later contributed funds for the establishment of the ʻImiloa Astronomy Center in Hilo.

Dr. Bakken responded by saying he wanted to interview Dwight first. He met with Dwight, and then endorsed him in the newspaper. Dwight won the Waimea district by an appreciable margin.

Dr. Max was extremely generous with his time, knowledge, and talents. He was interested in people, got along with anyone he befriended, and assimilated easily into the local culture. We are fortunate that he called Hawaiʻi his home for twenty-four years. When he passed away, he left a legacy of goodwill among his colleagues, employees, and friends. My life was enriched by knowing Max Goldberger, and I truly miss his company.

Larry Manliguis

Larry Manliguis, too, was a comrade-in-arms and a man of extraordinary integrity, compassion, and strength. Whether he was competing on the basketball court, fighting the war on poverty, or caring for his family, he exemplified the spirit of a true servant and warrior.

He served the county's disadvantaged residents as HCEOC's director of community services for thirty-one years and established a record of indelible achievements for others to try to replicate for decades. He created programs that dealt with human relations and helped thousands of disadvantaged people, from children to the elderly, achieve a better way of life.

Programs that flourished under his watch included the Language Arts Multicultural Program, which helped underachieving elementary school children improve their academic achievement; the dropout prevention program, which helped at-risk students graduate from high school; transportation services for the elderly and disabled; employment core services for low-income individuals and immigrants; the USDA surplus food distribution for low-income families; the low-income home energy assistance program; and the weatherization program.

There is no doubt in my mind that Larry's success was attributable to his character. He possessed, to an unusual degree, qualities that allowed him to execute his duties successfully without using intimidation or favoritism. He was unassuming, gentle, and yet firm in his conviction that everyone deserved a second chance in life. Always a gentleman, he never belittled his fellow man and he never used profanity. He treated everyone with respect, regardless of ethnicity and social status. Throughout the thirty-one years I knew him, I always felt privileged to be in his company.

The people miss him, the HCEOC staff misses him, and I miss him, both as a colleague and a friend. He was truly a heroic warrior.

Other Individuals

Jean Shimose, an aide in our LAMP program at Kapiʻolani Elementary School, is a great example of our employees' closeness with our clients.

After school one afternoon, there was a tragedy. One of the students in our program was playing with friends near his home when a playmate shot him between the eyes with a BB gun, and the student died. His very distressed mother, Mrs. Matsumoto, was a single parent who lived in Lanakila low-income housing, and she did not know what to do. She hesitated to inform the school principal or the regular classroom teacher because she didn't know them. But she knew Jean Shimose, our program aide, and she contacted her about the tragic incident. It exemplified the close relationship that existed between our staff and our client.

Jean was a warm and caring individual who commiserated well with all of her clients, students as well as parents, and developed lasting relationships with them. Later she became an employee of the University of Hawaiʻi at Hilo.

Barbara Dart, our Hāmākua district supervisor, was one-of-a-kind and the epitome of a community action supervisor. She took complete ownership of all the programs assigned to her and never missed anything; she passed on even the most trivial problems to Larry, the deputy director for community services, and then me, following the established chain of command, so that everyone was apprised of all problems.

She started with HCEOC just about when I was hired, and we both experienced the period of stress caused by the defunding notifications and the special conditions the federal government imposed.

Barbara knew every client in her district by name, which helped her become a powerful community advocate for mobilizing resources and community improvements. Her community meetings were always at full capacity. Her meetings were lively, with joking and congeniality, the discussions meaningful and productive, and she always attained consensus on serious programmatic matters.

On the lighter side, it's sometimes said that Portuguese women talk a lot, and Barbara did. If she telephoned in the evening, the call lasted more than thirty minutes, and after she said goodbye, the phone always rang again within fifteen seconds. Barbara would say she forgot something and ramble on for five minutes more. She never missed making that second phone call.

Barbara's strong and congenial relationship with community members was a powerful asset for political campaigning and she was an outstanding warrior in the war on poverty. She passed away in December 1998.

Chapter 16. Reorganizing the Grassroots, 1988

Bob Oshiro called me in early 1988 and said he wanted me to organize the Big Island's Democratic precincts to reduce party bickering around the primary election. In the past, when two or more Democratic candidates vied for the governorship, there had been animosity among the candidates' supporters. Bob was paving the way for a unified party in support of Governor Waihee in the 1990 gubernatorial campaign.

I assented and began recruiting Democratic party members; most of our grassroots campaigners were not members. I asked the county party chairman for membership application forms and more than a thousand of our grassroots people filled them out. I forwarded the completed applications forms to the party chairman, but we didn't hear back.

People started asking about their party membership cards, and I asked the chairman why it was taking so long. Even Jimmy Correia, the retired baseball coach, called me several times asking for his card.

The party chairman admitted that the membership application forms—more than a thousand of them—could not be found. They had been either misplaced or lost. I strongly suspected that someone feared our takeover of the party membership and had thrown away the application forms.

I asked the chairman for new membership application forms and he gave me all that he had on hand, which was seven hundred and fifty. Within a week, we resubmitted filled-out application forms, and finally, two weeks later, our grassroots members received their membership cards.

I called a meeting of the grassroots leaders and we reviewed attendance records at precinct meetings from two years before. We noticed that many precincts had only five or six people attending, and rarely were there more than fifteen. I recommended that for those precincts where only five or six people had been attending, we will bring in at least ten new party members; and where previously fifteen people had attended, will bring up to twenty people to the precinct meetings.

1988: Dukakis for President

Just two weeks prior to the Democratic precinct meetings, David Bradley, executive director of our national Community Action Foundation, called me from Washington, D.C. He requested that we vote for Massachusetts Governor Michael Dukakis as the nominee for U.S. President at the precinct caucuses.

I informed the grassroots of our preference for Michael Dukakis, and it turned out to be an easy victory. Dukakis won on the Big Island by eighty-two percent.

Soon after that, in May, I went as a delegate to the state Democratic convention on Maui, along with sixty other grassroots members also elected as delegates. Since many of our grassroots delegates were from low-income ranks, I asked people with frequent flyer miles on either Aloha or Hawaiian Airlines to donate plane tickets, and I asked for monetary donations for fifteen hotel rooms, which would accommodate four delegates to a room with two beds and two folding cots.

> Michael Stanley Dukakis was born November 3, 1933, in Brookline, Massachusetts. His Greek father had immigrated from Turkey, and his Vlach-Aromanian mother had immigrated from Greece. Dukakis graduated from Swarthmore College in 1955, was stationed in Korea while in the U.S. Army from 1955 to 1957, and then received a law degree from Harvard Law School in 1960. He was governor of Massachusetts from 1975 to 1979 and 1983 to 1991 and is the state's longest-serving governor. In 1988, he was the Democratic nominee for President.

I told my delegation we could not afford to pay for meals. But many of the candidates for various offices, including for U.S. Congress and the Senate, and incumbents such as the governor and lieutenant governor, had hotel hospitality suites where lavish meals were served, so there was no need to go out to restaurants. The Big Island Democratic party also had a hospitality suite that served breakfast.

The convention site was at a gymnasium. At the start of the convention, party platforms and resolutions were presented, each requiring a vote from the convention delegates.

I was asked to speak against one particular resolution—the early release from prison of James Albertini, who, in protest of war and nuclear weapons, broke the law by swimming toward a Navy warship anchored in Hilo Bay. As I waited to speak, I had a flashback that made me feel very uneasy—I remembered visiting the graves of my uncle, cousins, and other relatives killed in the atom bomb blast in Hiroshima when I was in the Army and visited family there. Many of the tombstones were fairly new, suggesting that the war reached that tranquil village only indirectly; that is, by killing villagers who had worked or gone to school there. It caused so much grief and suffering for their families.

I walked out of the gym to smoke a cigarette. I knew I could not speak against Jim Albertini.

When the resolution for Jim Albertini's early release passed, Roland Higashi smiled at me. "It's more important to puff on a cigarette than to testify against a human being," he said.

Jim Albertini and I went on to become good friends. In later years, he helped in our campaign for Dan Akaka by organizing community gatherings in Puna.

I noticed others campaigning for the delegate position to the National Democratic Convention, which would be held in Atlanta. When I saw Chuck Freedman and Governor Waihee, the governor said he would like me to be a delegate, and Chuck Freedman promised to campaign for me. The Hawaiians from Wai'anae said they would support me, too. With support from the governor, Chuck, the sixty Big Island grassroots delegates, and the Hawaiians from Wai'anae, I easily won a delegate seat to the National Convention.

Higher-ups in the party, and some elected officials, admonished me, saying I should wait for a signal from above before I began supporting a candidate for the presidency. They were referring to my having supported Dukakis; it seemed the decision-makers had someone else in mind. Our own U.S. Senator preferred Senator Gary Hart.

I attended the 1988 National Democratic Party Convention in Atlanta along with more than fifty thousand other delegates. Hawai'i had two delegations—one for Dukakis and another small entourage for Jesse

Jackson. Nationally known Democrats made speech after speech, and Hawai'i's Dukakis delegation occupied a reserved section very near to the stage. They could not only hear the speakers but could also see them close up. The delegates for Jackson, though, were seated far back and high in the stadium, and could not see the speakers well at all. They only saw tiny, unrecognizable people, like ants on the stage or the illustrations from the book *Gulliver's Travels*.

At the morning caucus, when Jesse Jackson was scheduled to speak, I suggested we yield our reserved seats to his delegates from Hawai'i so they could see him at close range. But to my dismay, no one from our delegation agreed. About twenty minutes before Jackson's speech, I climbed the steps to where Jackson's Hawai'i delegation sat and offered my pass to anyone wanting to hear and see Jackson up close. My offer was politely declined. I think they would have accepted if all the delegates could have been accommodated.

> Jesse Louis Jackson, Sr. (born Jesse Louis Burns; October 8, 1941) is an American civil rights activist and Baptist minister. He was a candidate for the Democratic presidential nomination in 1984 and 1988.

At the all-Hawai'i delegates meeting, held after the convention to finalize details about departing for home, I happened to sit next to Mililani Trask, who was a Jackson delegate. Mililani said she was establishing an office in Hilo called the Gibson Foundation for the Advancement of Native Hawaiians and that the first project she wanted to tackle was housing for Native Hawaiians. I informed her I was thinking about the same thing, and since I was a board member of the Hawai'i Public Housing Authority, I felt there might be an opportunity to work together on a housing project. We agreed to discuss it more back in Hilo. This encounter with Mililani was the beginning of a long-lasting friendship.

The Dukakis campaign splintered. Dukakis led in the polls at first, but gradually the Republican opponent George H.W. Bush started to close the gap.

The Bush team conducted relentless, negative campaigning and it was effective. One television ad in particular—about Willie Horton, who had been released from prison on a furlough program established by Governor Dukakis and then went on a rampage, committing violent crimes—was damaging. Every time it ran I cringed, and I became exasperated because the Dukakis team wasn't doing damage control. There was not a single rebuttal.

Dukakis stated that he would not succumb to mud-slinging and negative campaigning. Bush's incessant negative campaigning against Dukakis took its toll, and Bush eventually overtook Dukakis in the polls.

Negative campaigning has become the norm, the culture, of campaigning on the U.S. mainland and is successful. In Hawai'i, though, negative campaigning usually backfires and causes the candidate who mud-slings to lose.

It was certainly a disaster for Dukakis. He was defeated in every state except Massachusetts and Hawai'i, and in the District of Columbia.

After the campaign, Dukakis came to Honolulu as a visiting faculty member at the University of Hawai'i. Someone must have tipped him off, because at a gathering we both attended, Mr. and Mrs. Dukakis came by and shook my hand, thanking me for campaigning for him.

Back Home and Choosing Candidates

When we returned home from the 1988 National Convention, we concentrated our efforts on the re-election of various Big Island and state candidates who supported our programs. I requested our grassroots leaders include incumbent mayor Dante Carpenter on our list, and support his second term as mayor, even though for three consecutive years he had vetoed our transportation program before the County Council always unanimously restored it. I wanted to support him because Carpenter had helped us in other ways, such as with the Nā'ālehu Youth Center and negotiating with C. Brewer & Company for topsoil for our agricultural program.

The grassroots leaders were silent, and then Barbara Dart stood up and gave an eloquent and moving speech. I had preached to them, she said, about our agency's mission, and about how important it is that our clients have maximum participation in community affairs that affect their lives. I had insisted, she reminded me, that for our clients, transportation was a lifeline to living. Therefore, she said, we cannot have a mayor who believes the poor need not be provided with transportation. She said that we must have a mayor who is in agreement with our mission. Other leaders nodded in agreement. Barbara told me to look the other way.

I felt that our leaders had indeed learned to weave compassion for the poor into the fabric of human relationships. They wanted to be absolutely sure that a veto of our transportation program funds didn't happen again. I knew, though, that even if the mayor gave zero in his budget, the nine council members would have put it back in. It was an interesting dilemma; I felt as though the harness to the power of the grassroots had been just about severed, and they were about to take flight. We didn't support Dante Carpenter, who was popular, and he did not win. It was a shame we couldn't support him.

Our lack of support may have contributed to his demise. If so, it certainly demonstrated the power of the grassroots. All the candidates we supported won.

One of the successful new candidates we supported for the state House of Representatives was Jerry Chang, who was running for the Puna district seat. When he first came seeking our help, I did not know him and so I was reluctant. But when my friend Chabo Nagao asked me to help Jerry, I conceded, with the agreement of our Puna district grassroots leadership.

Jerry Chang later served as a Representative of the second district of Hilo. He became a staunch supporter of programs for the poor in his twenty-four years of service as a state legislator, and throughout his long career he helped us.

In January 1989, when the state legislature opened, I visited Representative Joseph Souki to express my sympathy at his having been toppled as Speaker of the House. Joe took it well, saying that he didn't mind being ousted as Speaker, but he did regret that only one honorable representative had offered his condolences. He told me he respected that person, Representative Dwight Takamine, because of it.

The House was reorganized under new leadership for the 1989 legislative session. Speaker of the House Calvin Say appointed Dwight Takamine as chairman of the Committee on Finance, the powerful money committee.

Dwight possessed unusual empathy for the economically disadvantaged, as had his father Yoshito, and he became a champion of our cause. I knew he would support us regarding legislative funding proposals for the poor, and he did. He got funding appropriated for eight programs, and Governor Waihee released the funds.

We were very fortunate to have Dwight looking after our state program funds until 2006.

He became a state senator in 2008, and in 2010, Governor Neil Abercrombie appointed him as director of the Department of Labor and Industrial Relations.

A Mover and Shaker

In February 1989, while I was advocating for program funds at the state legislature, several people told me to check out an article in *The Honolulu Advertiser*. I went to Dwight Takamine's office to glance at the paper and saw a nearly full-page article titled "Movers and Shakers in Politics."

There were photos of eight people: one from the U.S. Senator's office, two from the governor's office (including my friend Chuck Freedman), two from the Honolulu mayor's office, one from the Big Island mayor's office, one from the Supreme Court, and myself, stated as being from the grassroots.

"The cat's out of the bag," I thought.

I had remained fairly incognito and low profile during my fifteen years in the political realm, known only to our grassroots for political advocacy for the poor. But now, I realized, I might come under public scrutiny.

I convened a meeting of our grassroots leadership to review and ascertain that we all understood the allowable and unallowable political activities for non-profit organizations as stipulated in the Federal Hatch Act. In the event there was public scrutiny, I wanted to be sure that all political activities we conducted were allowable ones.

I told the leadership to expect many candidates asking for election help and stated that the leadership group would decide which candidates to support. I reminded the group that we were supporting twenty-two candidates: nineteen for council and state races, one U.S. senator after a six-year term of office, one U.S. representative after a two-year term of office, and the four-year term Hawaiʻi County mayor. I recommended that we vote on which candidates to support and only support those winning our vote.

The group agreed, and the outcome was a more unified and solidified grassroots power.

Conflict in the Ranks

There were two special elections in 1990, due to the deaths of both U.S. Senator Spark Matsunaga, who had helped us in the past, and Hawai'i County Mayor Bernard Akana.

Congressman Dan Akaka announced his candidacy for the U.S. Senate seat, and Stephen Yamashiro threw in his hat for Hawai'i County mayor.

For me, it was automatic that I would support Akaka and Yamashiro—Akaka, because I was his Big Island coordinator, and Yamashiro, because he helped us get full funding of our transportation program for four consecutive years.

Akaka's opponent was the seemingly formidable Republican state senator Pat Saiki, who represented an O'ahu district but was born and raised in Hilo. Lorraine Inouye, who was running in the special election for mayor of the Big Island, was also born and raised in Hilo and had many relatives and friends there.

We soon had a predicament on our hands regarding our overlapping Akaka and Yamashiro campaigns. It started when someone from California was hired as the new statewide coordinator for Akaka's campaign. He was said to have conducted a successful campaign for Senator Alan Cranston there, and right away I realized that his mainland style of campaigning was vastly different from ours. His was a shotgun approach, and he depended heavily on relentless TV media campaigning. He relegated grassroots activities to near-obscurity.

He told me to stop campaigning for Yamashiro for mayor. I told him that polls indicated Yamashiro was appreciably ahead in East Hawai'i, especially with support from Japanese voters for Akaka. I explained to him about our "We help you, you help us" approach of so many previous campaigns, which had resulted in victories. I told him that we were supporting twenty-two total candidates for various offices using this method, and that with this reciprocal agreement, we could muster thousands of Akaka supporters from among those of the twenty-one other candidates. But the statewide coordinator did not approve of this campaigning method.

He also admonished me for having visited Yamashiro's campaign headquarters. I'd stopped in there to say hello to my good friend, Patti Cook of Waimea, who was helping the Yamashiro campaign. Someone had me under surveillance and had reported my "suspicious movements" to campaign headquarters.

I told my grassroots leadership about the predicament I was in. They understood that I would not be able to support Yamashiro up front and said they would do the best they could.

I asked Dr. James Kurashige, a retired school principal, to take charge of Akaka headquarters. From past experience, I knew that Dr. Kurashige and his wife were honorable people who knew how to conduct a meaningful and victorious campaign. Dr. Kurashige accepted, and I was off the hook as far as the Honolulu leadership was concerned.

When Akaka came to the Big Island to campaign, I assured him he need not worry about our island, because he would win here. I advised him to spend his precious time on the other islands. Our grassroots supported Dan Akaka, John Waihee for governor, Ben Cayetano for lieutenant governor, two state senators, seven state representatives and nine council members, as well as partially supporting Steve Yamashiro for mayor, for a total of twenty-two candidates.

Daniel Akaka won. In fact, all our candidates won except for Stephen Yamashiro. Although he won in East Hawai'i, he lost in West Hawai'i.

I deeply lamented Stephen Yamashiro's loss in his bid to complete the mayoral term of Bernard Akana. He had been instrumental in saving our transportation program, not once but for four consecutive years. I told him that the next time he decided to run, he could definitely count on us.

The 1992 mayoral race—for a regular, four-year term—was upon us. I informed the grassroots leadership that we needed to prepare for the next election: again, Yamashiro for mayor. And I reminded them of the support he had given our transportation program.

Chapter 17. Stepping Down

After Dan Akaka became the first U.S. Senator of Hawaiian descent, I felt a real melding of spirits with the elderly sensei I'd met nearly fifty-eight years before, the one to whom I had vowed to be helpful to the Native Hawaiians. I felt so satisfied at having accomplished a step toward that end.

But then there was an unexpected turn of events. To my great surprise, Wayne Yamasaki, an official of HGEA, the largest public union, came to Hilo and informed me that Senator Akaka had appointed him as statewide chairman of the Akaka campaign organization. It was a complete shock to me since I had never met him nor even heard of him before.

Even more surprising was that he told me I was no longer Akaka's Big Island campaign coordinator, that he would soon be appointing my replacement, and that he had the authority to reorganize Akaka's statewide campaign organization.

Suddenly I flashed back to fifteen years before, and to our grassroots efforts that contributed emphatically to Akaka's victory in his first attempt for U.S. Congress. I also realized that Akaka had become well-known and respected throughout the state and that he could stay in Congress as long as he wanted.

I graciously agreed to being replaced and at the same time realized I felt a tremendous relief at being released from the responsibility of heading Akaka's campaign on the Big Island.

Now I could truly become part of our grassroots organization as a support arm for chosen candidates.

Akaka called, thanked me for my many years of support, and explained that he had given the new chairman full authority to run his campaign. I told him to rest assured that we would still support him and that anytime he needed help, we would always be prepared to assist him. I continued to correspond with his senatorial staff, and Akaka always supported our cause. Specifically, he voted for the Community Services Block Grant, the core funding for our existence as a Community Action Agency (CAA), and numerous other bills pertaining to CAAs.

In the meantime, on the community action front, we were fortunate to receive program funds from county, state, and federal governments. Everything seemed to be going our way. The only concern was our transportation program, as funding would be ending in just five months, on June 30, 1991. However, our grassroots leadership had contacted the nine county council members and obtained their commitment for funding; they assured us that our transportation funding would be appropriated.

Several months went by, and preparation for the 1992 elections was upon us. I kept reminding myself that we participated in political campaigns only for the mobilization of program funds for the poor, and to engage in affairs of the community affecting the lives of the poor, all in accordance with our mission. We stayed away from issues not related to the poor.

Our grassroots leadership met several times to select candidates to support. Twenty-one candidates were selected, but we emphasized the election of Stephen Yamashiro for mayor, for his help in restoring funds for our transportation program.

There were three candidates for the mayoral race. In addition to Stephen Yamashiro, it was incumbent mayor Lorraine Inouye, and Russell Kokubun.

Mayor Inouye had been victorious over Yamashiro less than two years before and therefore was a formidable candidate. Russell Kokubun was the chair of the county council, was a friend of the economically disadvantaged, and was also a friend who supported our programs. Early polls indicated that Inouye was leading and Kokubun was second. Yamashiro trailed in last place.

Our campaign for Yamashiro shifted into high gear. Roland Higashi, a veteran of many previous campaigns, became his campaign coordinator. He had capable assistants, many of whom were high school classmates and friends with long-lasting ties. The campaign steering committee was made up of individuals with vast experience in campaigning, including attorney Stanley Roehrig, and supervisory staff of the County Fire Department, Nelson Tsuji, Ed Bumatay, and Harry Onouye, to mention just a few. Harry was a veteran of many campaigns and recruited capable women volunteers to staff the campaign headquarters. He had campaigned for Akaka in the past and helped us with manpower for fundraising events. Later he retired with the rank of Assistant Fire Chief.

On the grassroots front, we organized community gatherings throughout the Big Island, twenty-four of them during the primary election and each one very well-attended. Harold Bugado, Larry Manliguis, and George Hanohano accompanied me to every one. The district grassroots leadership brought people to the gatherings. Many of the attendants were individuals who had participated in the storming of the county council to successfully advocate for restoring the funding for our transportation program.

The participants were treated to chili-and-rice dinners. George Hanohano, who transported the food in his van, became known as the "Chili Man" and was praised for the delicious chili meals at each gathering—though, actually, someone else prepared the chili meals.

Yamashiro attended all twenty-four community gatherings and shook hands with all of the grassroots people. As people headed home, I realized that most, if not all, who attended said they would vote for and campaign for Yamashiro.

Polls indicated that Mayor Inouye was ahead, especially among Filipino voters (who shared her ethnicity) and among Hawaiians (who, past election results showed, tended to vote for non-Japanese candidates. This is based on election outcomes of Keaukaha and Panaʻewa precincts, where the majority of residents were Hawaiian and a Japanese candidate had never won). Therefore, in addition to our grassroots community gatherings, we decided to hold two special gatherings, exclusively for Filipinos and Hawaiians.

For the Filipino gathering at the Seven Seas Lūʻau House, Santiago Gose was placed in charge. He set up voter registration tables and invited Filipino immigrants, whom he had helped become naturalized U.S. citizens, to attend the gathering. Nearly eight hundred new citizens turned up, proud to register to vote for the first time and to assimilate into this ethnically diverse community of people. The gathering was a success.

George Hanohano took charge of the Hawaiian gathering with a lūʻau also at the Seven Seas Lūʻau House. George was confident that he could fill the five hundred person capacity venue. I contacted Mililani Trask and asked if she would give a campaign speech for Stephen Yamashiro, and she gladly accepted. I wanted Mililani to speak because many Hawaiians respected her. The gathering was overwhelmingly well-attended. George Hanohano, with the help of Harry Onouye and his crew from the Fire Department, prepared food for six hundred people, but nearly a thousand attended and we ran out of food. We scrambled to the supermarket to buy prepared food, pastries, fruits and bread to make sandwiches and somehow we got by.

Roland Higashi and his steering committee were mindful of a recent poll indicating that Lorraine Inouye was still leading appreciably in West Hawaiʻi, although her lead was narrow in East Hawaiʻi, and decided to concentrate their efforts in East Hawaiʻi. The poll indicated that Yamashiro had positive upward movement, though West Hawaiʻi had no movement. They anticipated that vigorous campaigning in East Hawaiʻi would most likely overcome the deficit of West Hawaiʻi and win the election for Yamashiro.

Roland decided on a large fundraiser at the tennis stadium, not only to raise funds but also to demonstrate a force of support from the various ethnic groups.

He appointed Nelson Tsuji to head the event. Nelson came up with the idea of serving ethnic foods at separate booths: Hawaiian, Chinese, Korean, Japanese, Portuguese, Filipino, and American food. Roland gave me a thousand complimentary tickets to distribute to my grassroots, and the event was a success. More than three thousand people attended.

Within a few weeks of that event, with Yamashiro's campaign in full force, Yamashiro overtook Mayor Inouye and won the primary election.

The combined percentage of voters for the two losers was fifty-seven percent.

At the steering committee meeting following the primary election, many members felt that the general elections would be a pushover. The Green Party opponent, by the name of Davies, was practically unknown, to the extent that I cannot recall his first name. But just as many supporters expressed more cautious attitudes. Just four years before, Republican Bernard Akana, a perennial loser of many campaigns in his bid for various offices, had caused an upset victory over a seemingly formidable incumbent Democratic mayor in the general election. We couldn't take things for granted. We knew we had to continue to campaign hard.

Moreover, Yamashiro received forty-one percent of the votes in the

Stephen Yamashiro		15,000, or 41 percent
Lorraine Inouye		11,000, or 30 percent
Russell Kokubun		10,000, or 27 percent

primary election, less than the majority, while the opponents received a combined fifty-seven percent, meaning there were a hefty number of votes against Yamashiro.

Leading up to the general election, we again scheduled twenty-four community gatherings of our grassroots people, and again candidate Yamashiro attended all of them along with Larry Manliguis, Harold Bugado, George Hanohano, and me. The grassroots leadership of each district assembled the people and again we served chili and rice. The grassroots had gotten a taste of victory from the primaries and they were elated. They demonstrated an unusual degree of enthusiasm and zest for a victory in the general election.

Yamashiro received more than seventy percent of the votes, and won the election, of course. For the next eight years, our programs funded by the county government received support from the mayor and council members and were stable.

When he first became mayor, Yamashiro inherited a county government with a severe budget deficit. During his first term, he concentrated on balancing the budget, which he did expertly by freezing hiring, eliminating waste, and reducing the county work force, while still providing adequate services to the people of Hawai'i County. In his second term of office, he balanced the budget and ultimately left a large budget surplus for the next mayor.

Chapter 18. The Domino Effect

It was a difficult time for Hawai'i's sugar companies. Like dominoes, they went into bankruptcy, one after the other, and as a result there were mass layoffs. Living in Hawai'i, of course, being far from the mainland United States, means laid-off workers cannot job-search in adjacent states, as they would elsewhere. There were no established industries to take the place of sugar, or take on such a magnitude of workers, and it precipitated a horrendous job market.

Nearly twenty-five hundred skilled and unskilled workers were laid off—as many as fifteen hundred from the sugar plantations, and another thousand from sugar support businesses. Some laid-off employees found temporary relief by receiving unemployment insurance benefits.

And Santiago Gose helped some of them. Santiago, a naturalized U.S. citizen living in Puna, was a former ILWU steward who lost his union job. When Puna Sugar Company went into bankruptcy in the early 1990s and laid off hundreds of employees (foreshadowing the entire industry's demise within the decade), I hired Santiago at HCEOC to help those laid-off workers find jobs.

Fortunately, Hilo Coast Processing Company, which oversaw sugar plantations in Wainaku, Pāpa'ikou, and Honomū, was still operating, and it took on Puna Sugar Company's laid-off workers, though that would prove to be only a temporary measure. Next, we assigned Santiago to head up our immigrant services program, and he distinguished himself by helping nearly two thousand immigrants become naturalized U.S. citizens.

On the political front, he mustered naturalized U.S. citizens to support our candidates, and he became a part of our grassroots group.

Former immigrants, most of them Filipinos, were proud to exercise their right to vote, and they came out in droves to support our candidates.

Alex Gacula, another naturalized U.S. citizen from the Philippines, became the immigrant services specialist when Santiago left to work for Mayor Yamashiro. Alex carried on the work Santiago started—he helped nearly a thousand immigrants become naturalized citizens and helped solve some of the problems and needs of the immigrant population. He also participated in the grassroots group to support our political candidates.

What must have seemed, to outsiders looking in, like a Pacific paradise was nothing of the sort for a large segment of the Big Island's population in the 1990s. Conditions on the Big Island, as reported by the state departments of labor and industrial relations, human services and health, detailed the dire socioeconomic conditions.

The Big Island had:
- The highest unemployment rate of the four Hawai'i counties; more than eight percent (the other three counties had rates of four to six percent)
- The highest percentage of food stamp recipients in the state: twenty percent (though the county has only eleven percent of the state's population)
- The highest percent, in proportion to its population, of Temporary Assistance to Needy Families (TANF) recipients in the state (twenty-three percent)
- Both the lowest per capita income in the state and the state's highest cost of living

And perhaps because of these underlying problems, there were many surface problems, as well. The Big Island had the highest rates of child abuse, alcoholism, substance abuse, teen pregnancy, infant mortality, and suicide.

Although we were fairly successful in maintaining our efforts with state and county program funds, because the state government had instituted a fiscal austerity drive, we began to look to the federal government for resources.

On the national front, riding the wave of the campaign slogan "Contract with America," the House of Representatives came under the control of the Republicans. In 1996, there was talk of eliminating funding for the Community Services Block Grant (CSBG), which provided core funding for more than one thousand community action agencies across the nation. It seemed imminent that, after many attempts by Republican presidents throughout the years, the CSBG would finally be wiped out. The Republican-controlled Congress seemed to be taking on the task.

David Bradley, our executive director of the National Community Action Foundation, who had saved CSBG on many occasions, took on the challenge. He had an audience with Republican House Speaker Newt Gingrich. I do not know the details of their meeting, but after his forty-minute dialogue with Speaker Gingrich, CSBG was saved. Even more astonishing was the Speaker's agreement to increase CSBG funding by $100 million, to a total of $700 million.

David's accomplishment remains, to this day, unequalled. Because of his effort, community action agencies continue to be permanent institutions that serve the economically disadvantaged in our nation's communities and with an appreciable increase in funding, too. For a while, we were able to maintain our programs without drastic disruptions.

Taking a cue from David Bradley not to place all our eggs in one basket, I admit that although our grassroots had mostly supported Democratic candidates, we also successfully campaigned for certain Republicans that supported programs for the poor. Senator Richard Henderson, for instance, who was chair of the Senate Committee on Economic Development and supported us in appropriating program funds when Democratic and Republicans were merging to take leadership of the state Senate; Representative Virginia Isbell, who helped appropriate funds for the new homes we constructed in the poverty-stricken Hawaiian village of Miloliʻi; and Mayor Harry Kim, who continued to fund our programs from the county government.

With the Big Island in such a dire economic recession, I reassessed our programs and concluded that the only sure way to combat poverty was to enhance our job training and job placement activities through job creation and business development projects.

Conditions of poverty had existed since ancient times, I realized, and always would. There would always be people lacking the basic necessities of food, clothing, and shelter. Nowadays, these basic needs are provided by our benevolent government, numerous religious organizations, and non-profit organizations, including private foundations and philanthropists. But we reminded ourselves that human beings cannot be completely complacent and survive only on handouts. They must also have the opportunity to become economically self-sufficient—and to shift their negative attitudes toward work, family, and the community—so they can become social beings who are law-abiding, contributing citizens with human dignity.

To this end, we researched economic development grants, particularly those related to job training, job placement, job creation, and business development.

In the meantime, HCEOC had an opportunity for a business development venture. A group of Japanese entrepreneurs was proposing a business venture that catered to Japanese and other visitors.

Chapter 19. Opportunities

In the early 1990s, James Fukuda, who had graduated from Sophia University with me back in 1962, came to Hilo to visit his aging parents. He'd lived in Japan for nearly thirty years and had a lucrative business as a Japanese-to-English translator for large manufacturing and trading companies. He translated descriptive brochures, business letters, and comprehensive product research papers and was considered one of the top five translators in Japan. Many manufacturers and trading companies relied on his writing skills to accurately translate Japanese thoughts and significant meanings into comparable English—unlike work done by Japanese translators, whose dominant language was Japanese and who tended to translate verbatim.

He was in Hilo for five days, and we met every day and on several evenings.

I told him that our agency helped the poor by creating jobs and providing job training and placement, especially by changing negative attitudes toward work and family so participants became contributing citizens in the community.

He offered to help bring in program income for our organization and told me about the Japanese way of doing business. In Japan, they strictly followed the protocols of trust and respect, and relied upon introductions by influential persons within an entity, which was organized into a hierarchy of rank and authority. He had many friends within the companies he worked with, he told me, from section chief to division chief, department chief and, in some cases, president. He promised to refer me to respectful and influential individuals within those companies.

A few days after he returned home, he referred me to several individuals at trading companies and manufacturers that dealt with agricultural products. He believed that Hawai'i, being located in a subtropical zone, was well-suited for year-round production of agricultural products that were in demand in Japan.

Making Hay

One person he introduced me to was Kosuke Yamada, president of Yamada Trading Company, which was a major importer of baled hay for Japan's cattle industry. Within a few weeks, Mr. Yamada came to Hilo.

He told me he imported hay for Japanese cattle raisers from California, Oregon, and Washington. Cattle feed had become more and more in demand in Japan, commensurate with the increase in beef eating. But unlike the U.S., which has abundant pasture and grazing land, Japan has a mountainous topography; therefore, its farmers have to raise cattle in feedlots and bring feed to the cattle. Japan's dire need for cattle feed was well-known.

Immediately, I applied to the federal government for an economic development grant, and I received $400,000 for a cattle feed production project. After consulting with Mr. Yamada, we selected the fast-growing Sudan grass and planted the grass seeds on a two-acre test plot. He returned to Japan, planning to return when the Sudan grass was harvested.

The grass grew rapidly. By the time he returned to Hawai'i, it was three feet tall. In less than four months, the grass was an average of seven feet in height, and it was ready to be harvested.

It was definitely possible to have three harvests per year, we determined, unlike on the U.S. mainland, where one annual harvest was the norm (except in Southern California, which sometimes had two).

There was, however, one factor that threatened our hay production: Hawai'i's extremely high humidity. This was very different from the U.S. mainland, where humidity was low. On the mainland in the hot, dry months, grass was sun-dried to reach a moisture content of twelve percent, which prevents mildew in the hay.

Though he shipped in eight- by forty-foot sealed containers, Mr. Yamada had occasionally experienced tremendous losses due to mildew infestation in imported hay. He was alarmed by East Hawai'i's immensely rainy weather—more than three hundred twenty days per year—which made it impossible to dry grass in the sun except with a hay dryer, which cost more and pushed the project beyond profitability. It was Hilo's rain that ruined the hay venture.

Jute

Mr. Yamada came to Hilo again, though, and suggested an alternative crop: *Corchorus olitorius*, a member of the jute family. He brought us a sack of seeds, a gasoline-powered portable harvester, a motor for a hot-air dryer, and a hammer mill for powdering dried leaves and stems.

He contacted Takehaya Company, Ltd., Japan's second largest pharmaceutical company at the time, and my friend Jim Fukuda contacted Kikkoman Corporation, the world-renowned producer of soy sauce. Both companies expressed interest in a joint venture importing powdered jute, and Mr. Yamada would represent the two companies in their dealings with us.

We immediately sowed the seeds on a three-acre plot of land near Wainaku, which we leased from the land asset division of Kamehameha Schools, one of the Big Island's largest landowners.

To our amazement, the seeds sprouted in just a few days and were growing vigorously in a few weeks. Within three months, the succulent stems and leaves were ready to be harvested. To our delight, the green tea harvester Mr. Yamada provided made harvesting easy, and to our further elation, although jute was an annual plant, we discovered that by cropping the stems about three feet from the top, the plant sprouted new shoots that could be reharvested. This eliminated the need to replant after each harvest. I immediately requested an amendment to our grant award, from hay to jute production, and received approval from the federal funding source. We transferred our twenty low-income trainees from the hay project to the jute.

Jute's origin is traced to Africa, the Middle East, and some tropical Asian countries. There are approximately forty different varieties, each belonging to one of two categories. The one we were growing, *Corchorus olitorius*, was a garden-cultivated vegetable for human consumption and feed for animals. The plant grows to about eight feet in height, but for maximum leaf yield, it's cropped when it's about six to seven feet tall. In Japan it's known by its Egyptian name, Malukhiyah, and the leaves and stems contain a slick, mucilaginous substance similar to okra. The other type of jute, *Corchorus capsularis*, is grown for its fibers and is used to make ropes, sacks, and the like.

Jute production depends on warm temperatures and moisture in the soil. In Japan, the crop is harvested between July and early October, but in subtropical Hawai'i it can be harvested year-round. Awareness of jute was growing rapidly in Japan, and Hawai'i—with its pre-arranged markets—had the capacity and potential to become a major jute producer.

At Mr. Yamada's suggestion, we attached the tea leaf dryer to an eight- by twenty-foot metal container that could dry six tons of freshly harvested jute and installed an electric-powered dehumidifier to hasten the drying. We determined that we could dry the jute to less than a twelve percent moisture content in sixteen hours, starting at 4 p.m. one day and ending at 8 a.m. the next day. The dried jute was then hauled to our powdering and packaging plant, which was at a former kitchen of the old Hilo Memorial Hospital. There, the dried jute was turned into powder using the hammer mill Mr. Yamada had provided, and the powdered jute was placed into vacuum-sealed twenty kilogram nylon sacks.

Mr. Yamada showed me a nutritional analysis of one hundred grams of Japan-produced jute (by the Nagano Prefecture Laboratory of the Women's College of Nutrition):

Beta Carotene (I.U.) 10,826 I.U.
Potassium 920 mg
Calcium 410 mg
Iron 1.7 mg
Vitamin B1 0.72 mg
Vitamin B2 0.72 mg
Vitamin C 62 mg

A similar analysis of our Hawai'i-grown jute, by Food Products Laboratory of Portland, Oregon, showed ours to be far superior in nutrition:

Beta Carotene (I.U.) 23,423 IU

Potassium 3,112 mg

Calcium 1,659 mg

Iron 6.3 mg

Magnesium 311.11 mg

Copper 1.40 mg

Zinc 3.1 mg

Vitamin B1 2.6 mg

Vitamin B2 1.8 mg

Vitamin B3 6.74 mg

Vitamin B6 1.08 mg

Vitamin B12 0.81 mg

Vitamin C 6.28 mg

Mr. Yamada informed both Kikkoman Corporation and Takehaya Company, Ltd. of our jute analyses. We heard from Mr. Hiroyuki Yajitake, Kikkoman's manager of quality control of the biochemical division, and Dr. Nobuyuki Yamaji, of Kikkoman's research and development division, as well as Dr. Takaki Wakabayashi, director of technology development of Takehaya and Company, Ltd. They were all amazed and impressed with the results and within a few days, they all flew into Hilo.

They inspected our entire jute project—from planting, harvesting and processing, to packaging—and after suggesting minor corrections, they approved our project. A sample air shipment of one ton of powdered jute was sent to Kikkoman Corporation, followed by two shipments of two tons each. We were elated that our powdered jute export was going so well.

However, Dr. Wakabayashi returned to Hilo with a critical report: Our powdered jute was infested with *E. coli* bacteria and also contained traces of mercury.

Our new operation was not to be.

He explained that there are good and bad *E. coli*, and that our jute contained an *E. coli* that is found in the intestinal systems of all humans and is not harmful to people. But the health- and safety-conscious Japanese were leery at the mere mention of *E. coli*, he explained, and it would hinder marketing of the product.

He said that Kikkoman Corporation would eradicate the E. coli infestation from our powdered jute and ascertain the cost/benefit ratio of the eradication work, to determine whether the product could still be profitable.

As for the jute's trace mercury content, it was appreciably below the maximum allowable parts per million (ppm), and therefore acceptable. Public awareness of mercury poisoning, however, was high at the time, when people were eating fish caught in some of Japan's mercury-contaminated harbors. This would definitely affect product marketing, as would scrutiny from Japanese customs inspectors.

Dr. Wakabayashi explained that airborne mercury from Hawai'i Island's continuous eruption at Kīlauea Volcano might be the reason for the mercury content—some years lower, some years higher, but always in trace amounts that were below the allowed ppm. Kikkoman Corporation asked for two more shipments of powdered jute, of one ton each, to run more tests.

When the day of reckoning came, the cost of *E. coli* eradication was determined to be too high and the mercury content was deemed too unpredictable. The jute project had to be scrapped.

Dr. Wakabayashi wrote and apologetically explained that large, reputable companies in Japan strictly adhered to the health and safety of food products. He added that he had become fond of Hawai'i and its people during his short stay in Hilo. After he retired from Takehaya Company, he and his wife returned to Hilo and visited the field where the jute plants had grown, recollecting the efforts of all who participated.

We were grateful to Jim Fukuda for introducing us to reputable companies in Japan, and to Mr. Yamada for helping us expand our business contacts there.

We shifted our twenty jute project trainees to our agricultural training project. They cultivated fruits and vegetables for local markets, especially supermarkets; for our local production program, which prepared and sold meals to non-profit child care centers; and for the congregate meals program, operated throughout the county by the county government.

Tour Boat Business

In the late 1990s, Mr. Yamada called and said his son-in-law would be visiting Hilo and had a business proposition for me to consider.

His son-in-law was accompanied by a very rich individual, Mr. Yoshiteru Mishima, and two of Mr. Mishima's friends. The venture, a brainchild of Mr. Mishima's, would create a small new industry for visitors, as well as for the local population.

Mr. Mishima told me he noticed that visitors to the Big Island travel on tour buses, and that, especially on the east side of the island, there was a lack of visitor attractions. There were only long, monotonous bus rides, starting with a visit to Rainbow Falls in Hilo and Akaka Falls in Honomū. Then visitors viewed historical plantation communities along the coastal highway going north, or proceeded south to the Kīlauea Volcano area to see the eruption and lava flow. Many tour buses went around the island, some starting from Kona and others from Hilo, making round trips that encompassed the island's two hundred and sixty-mile perimeter.

He envisioned a sightseeing tour boat business, with an expansion to recreational endeavors, such as larger boats for parties, weddings, and other private gatherings. He proposed, at the onset, to launch a Kīlauea Volcano cruise, for visitors to view the spectacular molten river of lava that enters the ocean near Kalapana. In addition, he would offer a boat ride along the Hāmākua coast to historic Waipiʻo Valley, offering views of the waterfalls that intermittently cascade from the coastal cliffs.

Mr. Mishima and the others had stopped on Oʻahu before coming to Hilo, and he had already made a preliminary agreement there with a boat owner named Johann (Hans) Antal. Antal, a German citizen in his mid-thirties, was married to a Filipina-American woman and they lived in Hawaii Kai.

Mr. Mishima told me he gave Hans Antal $35,000 cash as a down payment. He wanted me to go to Oʻahu and meet with Antal to talk about transferring the boat to Hilo, berthing space for the boat, registration of a tour boat business, and Antal's proposal to become part of the venture. Mr. Mishima told me that he barely understood English, and he suspected the Japanese interpreter he hired had not accurately translated the specifics of his conversation with Antal. He needed to know Antal's proposal in detail.

I went to Hawaii Kai and met with Antal and his wife, who mentioned they were very good friends with Vicky Cayetano, the governor's wife. This lent credence to the couple's political and social status—though later, when I asked Mrs. Cayetano about them, she told me she had never met nor heard of them.

Antal proposed to work on a contract basis; he would operate the boat and be paid per trip. Before sailing for Hilo, Antal showed me the fifty-foot boat, the *Arisa*, which had a speed of thirty-five knots and would be used for the tour boat business. I returned to Hilo and informed Mr. Mishima of Antal's proposal.

The next step was to search for used boats on the West Coast—California, Oregon, or Washington—that would carry fifty to one hundred fifty passengers. We found there were many used boats in varying sizes available for sale there, and Mr. Mishima told us he would finance purchase of the boats. An inquiry about his cash assets—he'd made his fortune in the financial services business—revealed a high eight figures, implying he had between $50 and $99 million.

He wanted our agency to manage the business operation, and I recommended that our board of directors establish a for-profit corporation with stocks owned exclusively by HCEOC. The board approved my recommendation.

A profit-making corporation was established and called Hawai'i Human Enterprise Corporation. Mr. Mishima also established a Hawai'i corporation named Hilo Rainbow Corporation, and we both opened checking accounts at Central Pacific Bank.

In the meantime, the *Arisa* arrived with Hans Antal at the helm, and, with permission from the harbormaster, anchored at Reeds Bay next to Banyan Drive.

Mr. Mishima, Hans, our agency's attorney, and I met in the Naniloa Hotel's lobby. Hans agreed with everything Mr. Mishima proposed, but he seemed uneasy and checked his watch often. Finally he stood up and asked Mr. Mishima for a private conversation. Mr. Mishima obliged, but he asked me to listen in.

Hans demanded $25,000, cash or check, for delivering the *Arisa*. Mr. Mishima refused, stating that a deal was a deal. He vehemently objected to Hans's trying to breach their agreement of $35,000, which had been paid in advance for the boat's delivery. Hans left in a hurry and took a taxi to the airport.

After he left, our meeting continued. Mr. Mishima asked two of his Japanese friends to print brochures about the boat cruise allowing passengers to view the lava flow from the ocean and inform more than three hundred travel agencies throughout Japan that a new visitor industry had been established.

By chance, the owner of Naniloa Hotel, a Japanese national, was in town and we told him about our proposed venture. He was very supportive and recommended we use his small pier to berth the boat adjacent to the hotel, for easy boarding by his hotel guests. George Miyashiro, president of Jack's Tours, came by the hotel and expressed interest in hauling visitors to and from the embarkation site. From this brief encounter, an idea came about—to also position boats at the Kona and Kawaihae harbors, and transport visitors from hotels to piers via Jack's Tours buses.

We returned to my office, where Mr. Mishima told me he wanted to avoid the cumbersome red tape of doing business the American way, because he was not versed in English or U.S. business laws and regulations. He just wanted a simple arrangement where the boats would belong to his Hilo Rainbow Corporation, and he would take a percentage of the business's gross income. It would be up to our agency to make the venture successful.

This was unexpected luck for us, because all the start-up financing would be advanced by Mr. Mishima, including the millions of dollars for purchase of the boats.

Except that there was, suddenly, a catastrophe. Three days after the *Arisa* anchored at Reeds Bay, it was gone. We learned that its legal owner—who was not Hans Antal—had come to Hilo, fetched the boat and returned to Honolulu. Antal, it turned out, was only the boat's caretaker.

I immediately informed the police, the county prosecutor, and the state director of the Department of Commerce and Consumer Affairs about Hans Antal's swindle. The police searched the state for Mr. and Mrs. Johann Antal, but they seemed to have flown the coop with the $35,000. They were not found.

Mr. Mishima admitted that he let his guard down when he met Antal. He should have personally checked the *Arisa*'s ownership and registration documents, he said, instead of merely relying on the words of the Japanese interpreter. With the stoic demeanor of a samurai, however, he calmly accepted that the venture had ended in a debacle, and expressed regret for causing me disappointment.

He closed out the Hilo Rainbow Corporation bank account and notified the state Department of Commerce and Consumer Affairs of the corporation's termination. With the board of directors' approval, we placed our for-profit Hawai'i Human Enterprise Corporation in inactive status, but with the stipulation that it could be reactivated should a profit-making opportunity come up.

During his remaining days in Hilo, Mr. Mishima turned his attention to our programs. He was very interested in and eager to know about our programs for the poor—in particular, the HCEOC programs for high-risk, economically disadvantaged youth, and their positive outcomes. He returned to Japan after many hours of discussion about this. His last words were that he had become fond of how multiethnic groups lived so harmoniously in Hilo.

He has occasionally returned to visit again. Once, when he was in his mid-forties and I was seventy-two, he told me I was like a father to him. His father passed away when he was a child; perhaps that was why he felt that.

On another visit, I introduced him to Mayor Yamashiro and my friends Roland Higashi; Clifton Tsuji, who was, at the time, senior vice president of Central Pacific Bank; Yukio Takeya, president of Ala Kai Realty; and several others. When a group of our elected officials—including Mayor Yamashiro and his wife, Roland, Clifton, and some other business leaders—visited Japan, they were wined and dined by Mr. Mishima.

Later, he told me he started a youth program in the city of Kumamoto. And still later, I learned from Mr. Tsuji that Mr. Mishima established a program for low-income adults. I was elated to know that something so positive came from our encounter.

As for the profit-making Hawai'i Human Enterprise Corporation, it still exists but only on paper and in inactive status, without a penny having been spent and without expecting a single business transaction. To this day, HCEOC is the exclusive shareholder of its stocks.

More than ten years later, though, the local newspaper made a remark about our for-profit corporation in a front-page article about HCEOC, implying that something was amiss. If the reporter had asked us before running the article, he or she would have learned the bona fide, legitimate facts of the corporation.

> Two years after the newspaper article appeared, a blog published scathing fabrications about Hawaii Human Enterprise Corporation, implying that I owned it and was conducting my own business through it. I received two communications forewarning me of the blog post, saying that it could jeopardize future program funding, and I consulted an attorney friend. He advised me to hold off. If any harm came to me or our agency because of the blog post, he said, then he would file a lawsuit.

Chapter 20. Ben Cayetano for Governor, 1994

My commitment of support to Lieutenant Governor Ben Cayetano in his bid for governor came about one day in mid-1993, when Yoshito Takamine came to my office and told me, in high spirits, that he had presumptuously committed me to Ben's campaign for governor. He said Ben wanted to see me as soon as possible.

Yoshito and I went to Honolulu the next day, and as we sat down for a chat, Ben said he did want to run for governor in 1994, but if Senator Akaka was thinking of running, he would gladly yield to the Senator. Right then I realized that Ben was an honorable person, one who adhered to the silent protocol among politicians.

I assured him that Senator Akaka would not run for governor. It was the same reply I made to Governor John Waihee prior to his entering his race for governor. Both John and Ben were honorable men.

I told Ben that, in fact, Senator Akaka told me he really liked working in Congress and would not be running for governor because there was no continuity after two terms. Most importantly, he had not yet completed his work on the Akaka Bill for the recognition of Native Hawaiians, despite President Clinton's 1993 formal apology for the overthrow of the Hawaiian kingdom.

Ben started out speaking to me in Pidgin, bringing about a congeniality experienced only by local folks. He told me HCEOC operated good programs for the poor and that he supported our endeavors in bettering life for the economically disadvantaged. He was one of us, and I committed myself to supporting him.

Yoshito and I were invited to a dinner meeting that night at a Japanese restaurant in Waikīkī with Ben, Charlie Toguchi, and Dennis Matsunaga. Yoshito emphasized a grassroots campaign on the Big Island, and stressed the successes we'd had with grassroots campaigning for Ariyoshi and Waihee. Everyone agreed.

I was honored to be included in the conversation with this highest echelon of the Cayetano for Governor campaign organization, and I understood why Yoshito included me in the discussion of grassroots campaigns.

When I got back to Hilo, I told Yoshito I was committed to Ben Cayetano and that I would be talking to Roland Higashi to form a steering committee for Ben.

Roland called a meeting of his friends who had been involved in previous campaigns, all of them experienced in the art of campaigning. Stan Roehrig, the attorney, was appointed chair of the steering committee.

I informed my grassroots leadership of what had taken place and my reason for supporting Cayetano. Most members of this leadership group had supported Ariyoshi, the first Japanese-American; Waihee, the first Hawaiian-American; and now we had Ben Cayetano, the first Filipino-American. We were definitely becoming a contributing factor in the realization of a truly ethnically diverse society, in which any individual from any ethnicity could become governor of the state of Hawai'i.

The grassroots leadership unanimously agreed to support Ben Cayetano for governor.

Alfred (Butch) Castro and Gerald Demello, who were active in Governor Waihee's campaign, joined us, resulting in Waihee's group taking substantial roles in Cayetano's campaign.

There were six Democratic candidates in the primary election, with Cayetano being the only known candidate. He'd campaigned for the Lieutenant Governor's seat twice, successfully, and was well-known throughout the Islands with the support of labor, business, and grassroots groups. His would be an easy victory in the primaries.

In the general election, he campaigned against two candidates—Republican Pat Saiki and Independent Frank Fasi, running as a member of the Best Party. Both were well-known on O'ahu, but were never personally in contact with people on the Big Island.

Fasi had been mayor of the city and county of Honolulu many times, but he'd seldom visited the Big Island in previous campaigns. He relied heavily on media campaigning and was weak in grassroots and union support.

Saiki was born and raised in Hilo, and did campaign on the Big Island in 1990, when she ran unsuccessfully against Dan Akaka for the U.S. Senate seat.

With the combined efforts of business, labor, and the grassroots, Cayetano won and became the first Filipino governor of the state of Hawai'i. Our grassroots organization was proud to have contributed to his victory.

Our Big Island entourage attended the December 1994 inaugural festivities. Afterward, on a balcony of a hotel room suite, where Wayne Metcalf, Roland Higashi and I stood chatting, Governor Cayetano and Charles Toguchi came out onto the balcony. The governor, it seemed, was looking for me.

He offered me the position of executive director of the state Office of Community Services, but he needed to know immediately whether I would accept the position. It was an unexpected offer and an honor to be offered the high position—but after a moment of contemplation, and thinking about my staff and our grassroots organization, I politely declined. I told the governor I preferred to stay on the Big Island and that he was going to need me for reelection to his second term of office.

After the governor and Charlie left, Roland and Wayne told me I was a fool not to accept the position. I felt good, though, to know of the governor's high regard for me.

In January 1995, just about a month after the governor took office, I urgently needed to see him, and I pleaded with Representative Dwight Takamine to accompany me. He obliged. I needed to meet with the governor about the release of $2.5 million in Capital Improvement Funds for the plans, design, and construction of our office complex, which would house twenty-two of our programs for the poor.

Our complex would sit on five acres of state land on Rainbow Drive in Hilo, directly across the street from the entrance to Rainbow Falls, and the grant appropriation was to expire on June 30, 1995. That was only six months away. The state legislature had appropriated the funds in 1992, but they'd never been released.

Governor Cayetano responded by painting a gloomy picture of the state's economy. He said we were in an economic recession with a deficit that might climb to $300 million, and he faced the monumental task of balancing the budget. The state, he said, was essentially broke. The reason for the previous governor not releasing the funds suddenly dawned on me—it was due to the state's deficit.

The governor called Earl Anzai, the director of Budget and Finance. Earl said the same thing, that the state was broke, and everyone was quiet for a long five minutes. That was a long time that nothing was said.

Finally, Governor Cayetano spoke. "George, I'll release the money to you," he said. "You operate good programs for the disadvantaged people of the Big Island."

I was elated, but then I was curious about where the money would come from.

The governor told me he'd find the money through the expenditure leeway of the capital funds, not from general operating funds.

Within a year, the new office complex was constructed and ready for business.

Governor Cayetano was a courageous, honest, and straightforward individual. Faced with budget woes from the beginning of his reign, he took measures to cut state expenses, much to the dismay of public unions and educational institutions. He abolished nonproductive boards and commissions, imposed hiring freezes, cut the University of Hawai'i's budget, and imposed spending restrictions on all state departments, agencies, and offices, including travel restrictions. He imposed a clean sweep of all unnecessary expenditures, but all the cuts were justified and fair, as viewed by the general public for the common good, with the exception of the public unions.

Chapter 21. Cayetano's Second Term, 1998

There was a heated dialogue at a meeting of the Big Island Labor Alliance (BILA), of which I was a member. BILA, which was made up of public and private industrial unions, existed to promote the welfare of all working people.

This particular meeting had people bringing forth opinions as different as night and day. The room was filled with hostility. Public union members, particularly members of the Hawai'i Government Employees Association (HGEA), the state's largest union, vehemently criticized Governor Cayetano for his state budget cuts, and they demanded pay raises for their members—to the extent that some threatened to strike.

The private industrial unions kept silent, except for the courageous Eusebio "Bobo" Lapenia, head of the ILWU, who stood up and silenced the crowd. He presented another side of the predicament and pointed out that his union, realizing that the sugar plantations were near bankruptcy, was opting to take employee pay and fringe benefits cuts to save the industry; whereas the public unions were demanding pay raises from their employer, the state government, in the midst of a severe budget deficit.

I had no quarrel with the public unions; in a time of prosperity, I would have agreed with them. But I lamented that the discussion took place. It felt like a forewarning that the combined and complementary power of the triumvirate for political campaigning—business, labor, and the grassroots—was truly waning. I walked out of the labor alliance meeting feeling dejected and sad.

Stan Roehrig, who had chaired the previous campaign, called a meeting of the steering committee for Governor Cayetano. I felt a sense of gloom permeate the meeting. Previous campaign meetings had been filled with zest, but in this one, discussion turned to disgruntled public union employees, namely the largest two unions: HGEA, and the Hawaii State Teachers Association (HSTA). They were followed in size by the United Public Workers Union (UPWU) and University of Hawai'i Professional Assembly (UHPA).

I said that union members generally abide by the decision of union officials; however, where there are no pay raises, or their pay has been reduced, rank and file members do not abide by endorsement decisions made by union bosses. We took a wait-and-see attitude regarding whether the union members would come our way or campaign against us.

We knew Cayetano would breeze through the primary, as his opponents were unknown. The battle would be in the general election where his opponent, Linda Lingle, was a former Republican mayor of Maui County. She was a popular mayor, elected to office for two terms, and fairly well-known throughout the state. We aimed our campaign activities toward the general election and against Lingle.

A few months later, early statewide polls indicated that Lingle was leading by twenty-five percent overall. On the Big Island, her lead over Cayetano was more than thirty-five percent. We were facing a formidable opponent.

My prediction, I told our grassroots leadership, was that Cayetano winning a second term would be a very steep uphill battle. Although I expected the public unions would rubber-stamp his endorsement, I didn't think their rank-and-file members—who were disgruntled over his fiscal austerity drive that was affecting their take-home pay—would vote for him. Ben Cayetano was a casualty of those union politics gone amok in his bid for a second term of office. With the exception of a few pro-Democrat businessmen, I explained, the business sector would likely support Linda Lingle because of her pro-business stand.

Our grassroots leaders stubbornly and unanimously opted to back him anyway, regardless of the likely outcome, because he was known to be a supporter of all people, particularly the poor and needy. Cayetano's campaign steering committee met to discuss the latest poll, which indicated a miserable showing—he was more than thirty percentage points behind Lingle, without any improvement in poll numbers.

I told Roland Higashi I was willing to go around the island with Vicky Cayetano if she could find time for a whistle-stop campaign like we organized for Jean Ariyoshi in 1974. Roland and the steering committee members agreed.

I called Cayetano's campaign headquarters in Honolulu and Vicky Cayetano agreed to come. We set up a schedule, comprised of community gatherings not to exceed thirty minutes each. Most were well-attended. Our normal campaign team of Harold Bugado, George Hanohano, Larry Manliguis, and myself accompanied her. Mary Matayoshi, the wife of former mayor Herbert Matayoshi, joined us, too.

At the Kohala senior center gathering, Mrs. Cayetano was asked to play the piano and sing a song. She did. The crowd was very pleased and felt warm congeniality with the governor's wife. At a Kona public housing project, residents complained that the housing management was not picking up rubbish and receptacles were overflowing. She immediately called the Hawai'i Housing Authority and remedied the situation. The residents there were impressed with her for taking immediate corrective action.

She stayed overnight at a Kona hotel. Early the next morning, she stopped in Nā'ālehu and Pāhala, and then went on to Kea'au and elsewhere in Puna. By noon, she was back at her husband's campaign headquarters in Hilo. The whistle-stop meetings were a success.

To drum up more support, Roland recommended we hold a gathering for Ben Cayetano, similar to the one we'd held for Mayor Yamashiro in 1992, when we gathered more than three thousand voters at the tennis stadium. We agreed, and arranged entertainment by the popular Filipino show band The Society of Seven. To our amazement, more than five thousand people showed up. It was the largest crowd in the history of campaign gatherings in Hawai'i County.

I looked around the crowd with some apprehension, though. Conspicuously absent were the public employees that usually came to political gatherings, and the haole group was also sparsely represented. Only local grassroots and senior citizens, especially Filipinos, were there in large numbers. On the one hand, the gathering was a tremendous success, but on the other hand, without the usual participation from public and private sector union members, I feared the worst.

It was rubbing salt in the wound, and I recoiled, when I saw public union members—many of them my friends, such as school teachers—waving signs for the Republican candidate Linda Lingle and wearing Lingle T-shirts on the front street of Hilo.

It was a tremendous relief on Election Day when Cayetano's campaign coordinator Charles Toguchi appeared on television to read from the last printouts. He declared Ben Cayetano the winner, by a squeaker.

It was the first time our Big Island grassroots candidate lost on our own island, and he lost by a whopping five thousand votes. It was also, unfortunately, the start of our tripartite effort crumbling.

But the fact that Governor Cayetano was ultimately elected to his second term of office gave our grassroots some solace. All the other candidates we supported won, as well.

I could not blame the members of the public unions for being against Cayetano. It was a pocketbook issue. He was a governor who executed his duty to serve all people of the state without fear or favoritism, but with fairness and equality for all people, and he came into office at a very difficult time economically; however, when he left office, he left the next governor a balanced budget.

Aaron Chung ran for Hawai'i County Council in 1998 and his district included the Hawaiian Home Lands of Keaukaha and Pana'ewa. His opponent was a Hawaiian Republican who lived in Keaukaha.

Keaukaha resident George Hanohano, one of our grassroots leaders, took it upon himself to campaign for young Aaron, even taking a five-day vacation from work to garner votes by asking his relatives and friends in Keaukaha and Pana'ewa to help Aaron. By the end of the fifth day, he had amassed more than fifteen hundred votes expressing support for Aaron through relative-to-relative and friend-to-friend contacts. Aaron was elected to the County Council and became chair of the Finance Committee.

He asked me to go with him to see the governor about releasing capital improvement funds for construction of the Kawānanakoa Center in Keaukaha, which would consist of a gym, classrooms, and facilities for arts and crafts. We made an appointment with the governor and flew to Honolulu. The governor asked Sam Callejo, director of Accounting and General Services, to be present at our meeting, as well.

Governor Cayetano only asked us one question: "Is the Center for public use?"

When Aaron and I replied in the affirmative, the governor turned to Sam and told him to release the funds.

Aaron and I became trusted friends and became able to freely discuss confidential matters. He was a standout supporter of our program, and I was happy to be able to help him with the release of funds for Keaukaha's much-needed Kawānanakoa Center.

Chapter 22. Grants

When the 1998 election was over, I thought about the old saying, "Politics makes strange bedfellows." In the fleeting moments of campaigning, friends sometimes became adversaries and, likewise, former foes became friends. I knew that many of my public union friends had campaigned for our opponent, hoping for better pay and benefits that would improve their lives, and I respected them for that. They had their reasons, just as I had mine. It's like a sports tournament where one team competes against another team, but afterward the winners and losers come together and continue their friendships.

I thought about how elections and politicians come and go, but friends are for a lifetime.

On the community action program front, we desperately wanted more program funds, commensurate with the significant population of economically disadvantaged on our island, and looked to the federal government for large grants. We came upon a federal grant announcement by the U.S. Department of Labor in the *Federal Register*, soliciting grant proposals for a welfare-to-work program.

I read the grant's requirements and guidelines over and over, more than twenty times, and with each reading I made more notes. I was determined to try for a hefty, $4.2 million grant, although I realized we would face formidable competition from higher educational institutions and large non-profit corporations. In many cases, they hired university faculty members to write grant proposals, or professionals who made a living writing grants and who earned five percent or more of the grant amount awarded.

I suddenly realized I was getting old. I was seventy-two, and felt like

I couldn't endure the strenuous task of putting together a fundable grant application much longer, while having to put aside my major duties as an executive director. We had a ninety-eight percent success rate and had received many grants, but suddenly I doubted whether I could keep it all up.

My grant application process had always consisted of gathering data for needs assessments, writing the narrative and developing a budget with the assistance of our fiscal officer, Toshie Miyasaki. I wrote, reviewed, corrected, rewrote, and then passed it to Joyce Madamba to type and retype until we got to the final printout. Joyce was the only one who could type the proposal from my handwritten and disastrously illegible draft. It was time-consuming to solicit letters of commitment for cost-sharing and matching funds from public and private agencies, but we needed such letters that detailed contributions to our proposed programs in the form of cash or other tangible in-kind contributions of property or manpower.

It was strenuous. We were all swamped with work and could not spare time for grant writing during our normal work hours, except for some typing by Joyce and budget review by Toshie. Mostly, grant preparation work was extra work that took place after everything else.

The Schedule

A grant's narrative section was typically fifty-five single-spaced pages, and the submission deadline was usually on a Monday at 4:30 p.m. Eastern Standard Time (EST). That meant electronically submitting our application by 10:30 a.m. Hawai'i Standard Time (HST).

We usually started on a Wednesday at 5 p.m., after our regular work hours, and continued until midnight. Then it was the same hours on Thursday and Friday, and then from 9 a.m. to midnight on Saturday. On Sunday, we started at 9 a.m. and worked around-the-clock until 8 a.m. Monday morning.

Within those five days, I smoked ten packs of cigarettes, skipped lunch, drank gallons of coffee, and ate snacks at the nearby McDonald's for supper. I usually lost five pounds of body weight.

To ease some of the burden, now that it was starting to feel onerous, I decided to form a grant development team. I hand-picked staff members

I felt were capable of forming a strong team to tackle the welfare-to-work grant application. This included Larry Manliguis, deputy director for community services; Toshie Miyasaki, fiscal officer; Jessica Yamamoto, program manager; and Joyce Madamba, computer operator. I invited Dr. Max Goldberger to join our team as well.

Jessica gathered data from the state Department of Health, Labor, Human Services and Education about substance abuse, unemployment, poverty conditions, and high school dropout rates on the Big Island. She also made comparisons with data from other Hawai'i counties in preparation for the needs assessment narrative.

Joyce's work consisted of typing and retyping, designing charts, creating a table of contents, numbering pages, copying them, and putting the proposal contents in order.

Larry volunteered to design the schedule of implementation for the seven program projects that would be under his control. He was also assigned to write the monitoring and evaluation procedures.

Dr. Max wrote the highly technical aspects of the renewable energy training component of one project.

I wrote the analysis of needs and a description of the eight projects we decided upon for our welfare-to-work program, and included objectives and interventions for each. I also took on the time-consuming task of soliciting commitments from public and private agencies for cost-sharing and matching funds of cash and in-kind contributions.

I told the team to remember we weren't writing a literary masterpiece and to use adverbs and adjectives only when needed to emphasize a point. Most importantly, I told them, write at a tenth-grade vocabulary level so reviewers could scan our proposal easily and without hesitation. This was based on my own experience as a grant reviewer years before. The grant review had been held at a Virginia hotel with thirty reviewers who were university faculty members, experienced service providers, and individuals possessing grant review expertise. I was classified as a service provider.

After an orientation meeting, we were separated into ten teams of three. Each team reviewed and scored twenty-four applications within forty-eight-hours. Each reviewer received twenty-four grant applications and a checklist of elements to review in sequential order. The reviewers graded each element and tallied them on the score sheet. From that experience, I had devised my own checklist.

Delay

We completed our welfare-to-work grant application in a little more than a month. It turned out we needed it all. We were down to the wire on meeting the deadline because of hold-ups along the way. We needed to forward our proposal to our county mayor for his signature on a statement of support letter; we needed a signed certification of consultation with the Hawai'i County Private Industry Council (HCPIC, which was the forerunner of the Hawai'i County Workforce Investment Board); and we also needed a signed certification of consultation from the director of the state Department of Labor and Industrial Relations.

HCPIC did not approve our application right away. The council received three applications to review and discussed whether to approve all three or select just one. One member wanted to select a single application.

I testified that the sole objective of the grant proposals was to bring money to the Big Island, and that the people of the Big Island would benefit regardless of who received the grant. I strongly recommended that HCPIC approve all three applications, because then the chance of our county receiving a grant award would increase threefold. After prolonged discussion, the matter was postponed. At their meeting the following month, only seven days before the deadline, all three applications were approved and the board chairman signed the certification of consultation.

We received the signed certification of consultation we needed from the state Department of Labor and Industrial Relations just five days before the deadline.

We also had trouble getting the statement of support we needed from Mayor Steven Yamashiro. He had assured me he would sign the statement before leaving for an out-of-town conference, but he did not. He was not scheduled to return to work until Monday, which was our deadline.

He actually returned to the Big Island on Sunday evening. I called his home and told him we desperately needed his signature. He told me to come to his office the next morning at 8 a.m. to pick up the signed statement. I got there at 7:30 a.m., just as he arrived. He signed the statement, and I rushed it to our office.

Jessica was sitting at the computer while I inserted the mayor's statement into the application. It was 8:15 a.m. and the grant application was due by 10:30 a.m. She started the transmission.

Worry

To our total dismay, the electricity went out. The town of Hilo was unexpectedly blacked out.

When the electricity came back on about fifteen minutes later, Jessica started sending our application again—but then the power went out again, this time just for a few minutes. When it came back on, she started sending our application a third time. We were getting down to the wire, and we gathered nervously around her and the computer.

Finally, thankfully, the application went through. When the words "Transmission Completed" appeared on the screen, I looked at the clock. It was 10:29:39 a.m. in Hawai'i, which was 4:29:39 p.m. on the East Coast. We had met the deadline with only twenty-one seconds to spare.

Our grant development team let out a shout, "Hurrah!" as if we'd actually been awarded the grant, not just gotten it submitted on time. Larry pointed out that twenty-one is a lucky number and said he had a premonition that we would receive the grant. Everyone agreed. I was elated and so grateful to realize we had such a committed grant development team.

That was July 1998 when we submitted the grant application, for a program that would commence in January 1999, if it was funded, and run for two years. But then the U.S. Department of Labor did not announce the grant awards as expected. We were on the verge of giving up when Congresswoman Patsy Mink finally called and, lo and behold, she congratulated me and said our application had been funded for $4.2 million. Later I learned that when a federal grant is awarded, the district congressional office is notified first, and then the news is disseminated by the congressional office to the media and the public. We learned that there had been twelve applications from the state of Hawai'i. Our application was the only one funded.

I immediately called a quick meeting of our grant development team to let everyone know we had been awarded the grant. Everyone was ecstatic and one team member even cried tears of joy. I took everybody out to dinner and we had a small celebration. I know we all felt proud to be a part of that successful team and such great satisfaction about the grant being awarded.

In addition to that $4.2 million federal grant award for our welfare-to-work program, we mobilized more than $9 million in cash contributions for cost-sharing and matching funds. The largest contribution came from the state Department of Human Services. We were grateful to director Susan Chandler, who committed more than $8 million from her First to Work program for stipends to clients of the Temporary Assistance to Needy Families (TANF) program, which tremendously aided in our application's success. Other contributions came from the state Office of Community Services, the Workforce Development division of the Department of Labor and Industrial Relations, and Alu Like Incorporated, for a total of $1 million. Total funds for our two-year program swelled to a whopping $13 million.

We also received fifteen letters committing support from other private and public organizations, including Hawai'i Community College and the University of Hawai'i.

The Projects

Our eight projects were:
- Incubator Kitchens. Three public health-certified incubator kitchens, located in three communities, where welfare clients would learn to produce confectionary food products, preserved fruits, and vegetables for wholesaling to supermarkets and other retail outlets. One kitchen, at Hakalau, was the former and well-known Fujii Bakery on in-kind lease to us. Another was a fairly new incubator kitchen at Pa'auilo that was transferred to us for lack of operational funds. The Honoka'a kitchen, formerly the Honoka'a Hospital kitchen, was also on in-kind lease to us.
- Agricultural Training. The state Department of Land and Natural Resources leased us fifty acres of land at the end of Kūkūau Street, beyond Sunrise Ridge in Hilo, for training welfare clients to cultivate agricultural products. We would then export these to Honolulu through Hilo Products, Inc., and sell them to our food service program, which prepared and sold

meals to the County Congregate Meals, Meals on Wheels, our preschool Head Start program, supermarkets and other retail outlets. A separate project was honeybee keeping. Two years of year-round honey production would train participants to become independent beekeepers and earn supplemental income. George Hanohano would manage the agricultural training projects.

- Carpentry Training. In agreement with the Carpenters Union Local 745, we would establish a carpentry training project with a licensed contractor, former Hawai'i Community College carpentry instructor Carl Shoji, overseeing it. Under Carl's leadership, trainees would learn to use carpentry tools and equipment and help participants in our self-help housing program (especially single-parent mothers, elderly, and disabled persons) build their own homes. The aim was for participants to progress in the building trade from apprentice to journeyman, as sanctioned by the Carpenters Union Local 745. Once trained, participants would be able to construct their own homes.
- Computer Learning Centers. We would establish centers at the Pāhoa field office by renting an annex building of a service station in Pāhoa, and at a former Laupāhoehoe infirmary. The goal was to increase the employability of female TANF program clients, all single mothers. Jessica Yamamoto would manage the project.
- Renewable Energy Project. Under the guidance of Dr. Max Goldberger, this project would create renewable energy devices such as solar water heaters, electricity generation by photovoltaic cells, parabolic mirrors for solar heat generation to power electric modules, steam generation for steam engines, and desalination of seawater. Under Dr. Max and other experienced supervisors, TANF recipients would learn to operate electric welders, lathes, and other machinery and equipment for fabricating energy devices.
- Confectionary Gift Products Manufacturing and Marketing Training. A public health-certified, 3,600-square-foot kitchen was built at our central office property. In addition to learning to produce confectionary gift items, such as candies and baked

goods using honey, chocolate, macadamia nuts, shredded coconuts, and tropical fruits, TANF clients would also learn to use equipment. A consultant would be hired for six months to assist George Hanohano in setting up the operation.
- Gift Shop. Directly across the street from the famous Rainbow Falls, one of Hilo's few visitor attractions, we would establish a small gift shop at the entrance to our central office facilities. More than fifty tour buses and many visitors in rental cars visit Rainbow Falls every day of the year, more than two thousand visitors per day. The Rainbow Falls area also has government facilities on public land, such as the hospital, county prosecutor's office, county annex buildings, and non-profit organizations. Private commercial enterprises could not be established, so there was no commercial business competition there.
- Open Market. A three-acre parcel of land at the upper portion of our central office complex was slated for establishing an open market. It would target both visitors and residents and feature local vendors selling their art and craft wares from assigned booths. Our sales clerk trainees would also sell our confectionary gift items.

At the onset of implementing the welfare-to-work program, and in order for the program to truly benefit TANF clients, I pondered several things we would need to provide to overcome barriers to employment.

First, I considered the welfare situation in Hawai'i. The state, I knew, had some of the nation's most liberal benefits. A typical family of four, with two children under thirteen, received monthly cash benefits of $687, food stamps worth $660, medical benefits of $659, transportation expenses of $100, and childcare benefits of $650 for each child, for a total of $2,756 per month or $33,072 per year. They also received a housing allowance. The perennial welfare recipient had become complacent and was fairly satisfied with a life on government assistance.

Also, many were among the least job-ready and the least motivated to learn job skills and seek employment. But a recent change in the law required incremental cuts in benefits after sixteen months, and that compelled welfare recipients to start looking for work.

The majority of our clients were single mothers who had never worked before; many had gotten pregnant while in high school, and then left school without graduating to raise her child.

What We Tried to Teach

I knew that what was most critical was that our clients learn to accept employment as a new way of life—to go from living on handouts to becoming contributing citizens with a purpose in life, so that they would break the cycle and their own children would not also grow up in poverty.

We recruited TANF clients in incremental stages. Each project held a five-day workshop in the classroom, covering topics that ranged from positive attitude development to improving self-image and functioning. Our goal was for a complete turnaround from a welfare way of life to a working one.

Clients learned about the team approach and the chain of command that gets things done. They learned about subordinate-superior relationships and how a team is organized. Each member knew exactly whom to report to when a problem arose, so that all in the chain were kept aware of a project's progress, and they knew that remedial actions were taken if problems arose. It was satisfying to see disheartened team members receiving encouragement from fellow team members to persevere in the face of discouragement. Periodic workshops on developing a positive attitude were held throughout a project's duration.

I assumed that even the least job-ready client could handle our assigned tasks, because working indoors only requires dextrous hands to do tasks that can easily be learned, and the outside work on our mechanized, renewable energy and farm work projects just required easy physical effort. That first year, our project enrolled three hundred TANF clients, and we enrolled two hundred more clients the second year. Those five hundred clients fulfilled our obligation to the grantor.

Of the five hundred clients, we were very pleased that ultimately we were able to place three hundred and eighty of them in unsubsidized positions such as sales clerks, computer operators, farm workers, office workers, truck drivers, forklift operators, arc welders, and crane operators in the visitor, agricultural, and building industries. Some found jobs in government and retail business. Sixty of our clients later went on to pursue higher education at Hawai'i Community College and fifteen enrolled at the University of Hawai'i at Hilo.

One of our employees was Shirley Filoteo, a former welfare recipient who became a kitchen supervisor in our Rainbow Falls Connection. She was in charge of the Hilo kitchen, where they produced fifteen varieties of lavosh for sale at supermarkets and various specialty stores, including sweet potato, ulu, mango butto, macadamia nut, garlic, and more.

Before starting with our program, she had never held a job. "I never thought I would ever be a supervisor someplace," she said. Not only that, but Filoteo established credit, bought a car, and was working toward buying a house. She eventually went on to a better-paying job; too bad for the Rainbow Falls Conection, but it was ultimately the goal of the program—getting the clients self-supporting and into the workforce. She was just one of many success stories.

Some notable highlights of our projects were:

- Agricultural Training. Hilo Products, Inc., which exported Big Island agricultural products to Honolulu, told me we became the largest producer of green onions for the Honolulu market.
- Carpentry Training. With the help of our project trainees, and through our self-help housing project, we constructed twenty-eight homes for single mothers, elderly, the disabled, and the low-income in Keaukaha and Pana'ewa.
- Computer Learning. Previously, classified ads for office workers required that applicants "be able to type sixty words per minute," but that had evolved to "must be able to operate a computer." Our trainees became highly competitive for any job requiring computer skills. All forty graduates of our computer learning project found jobs.
- Manufacturing and marketing of Confectionary Gift Products. The U.S. Department of Defense announced that it was soliciting locally made products for sale at military commissaries, but that a panel of judges must first approve the products. More than a hundred producers sought approval. I sent Jessica Yamamoto with thirteen samples of our products and, to our surprise, the judges approved all thirteen. After that, orders from distributors throughout the state increased.

Locally, we were grateful to Barry Taniguchi and Derek Kurisu, president and executive vice president, respectively, of KTA Super Stores, for carrying our products in their supermarket chain. KTA Super Stores is the preferred supermarket for many local folks because it caters to customers desiring local foods and Asian flavors. KTA was also considerate of its customers. When there was an impending hurricane, for example, and Civil Defense announced that the public should stockpile emergency items such as batteries for flashlights, bottled water, and food, KTA sold items at their usual prices or actually lowered their prices. Alert, low-income housewives told us that other stores raised their prices.

- Open Market. Our Open Market started rather slowly until Michael Free, general manager of the tour bus company Roberts Hawaii, came from Kona and observed it. He liked what he saw: hula dancers entertaining visitors with Hawaiian dance, and young ladies singing Hawaiian songs, much to the enjoyment of visitors. Mr. Free told me that unlike other tour stops that were strictly commercial, our Open Market had a cultural flavor. He told me he would instruct his company's tour bus drivers to make our Open Market an official tour stop, and that increased our attendance tenfold. It was a joyous moment when the Open Market's supervisor Mike Leopoldino burst into my office shouting, "We reached a thousand and twenty!" He was holding a clicker device that counted the number of visitors entering the Open Market. It was only 3 p.m., and there were still several more hours before closing.

Riding that streak of good fortune, we looked for more program funds from the state government, even though the state was still within the governor's fiscal austerity drive. We applied for six grant-in-aid funds of approximately $1.5 million total to continue operating our other programs.

Representative Dwight Takamine was chair of the House Finance Committee at the time. He stood for fairness for all, regardless of one's social or economic standings, and was committed to allocating funds for worthy endeavors that helped the state's disadvantaged. I boldly testified at various House committee hearings in support of our requests and assumed his committee would approve our funding requests. I was right; finally, the House Committee on Finance did approve all of our requested funds.

We also needed the approval, though, of the Committee on Ways and Means, the Senate money committee that Senator Ann Kobayashi chaired. She was friends with Mike Amii, whom I had befriended years before, and he gladly accompanied me to see her. She committed to supporting our funding requests.

After I testified at various Senate committee hearings, our grant requests were all approved, and the House and Senate appropriated the funds. Governor Cayetano released the funds effective July 1, 1999.

At that point we had ample resources and no anxiety about how to fund our programs, so for a while we coasted along comfortably. We implemented our community service and welfare-to-work programs and they ran for nearly three years. Our welfare-to-work program was supposed to end on December 31, 2000, after two years, but we continued to employ our former welfare clients beyond the grant contract period because we anticipated that our income-producing, self-supporting projects would become reality. But it was not to be—only because of an unforseen disaster that was yet to come.

A Memorable Episode

In 2000, Larry Manliguis kept telling me that Hilo High's basketball team was the most exceptional team he had ever coached. Its team members, he said, were well-disciplined and motivated in the classroom, as well as on the basketball court. When we talked over lunch, the conversation always included his Vikings team.

One day he asked me if I knew my counterpart at the Economic Opportunity Board in Clark County, Nevada. I did. The executive director there was Jim Tyree, and I'd befriended him while attending conferences on the U.S. mainland. In fact, Jim had donated four buses in good operating condition to our agency.

Larry begged me to contact Jim. He wanted me to ask if the basketball coaches in Nevada high schools would include the Hilo High Vikings in their upcoming tournament.

I called Jim right away. He had some doubts whether the Vikings were good enough to take on the Nevada teams, because their high school players were as good as college kids. But I assured Jim that our boys were just as good and could compete, telling him the Vikings were crowned champions of the Big Island for the past ten consecutive years. He was convinced, crashed the high school coaches' meeting and presented the proposition to include the Vikings in their tournament. The Nevada coaches agreed, and the one in charge of the tournament called Larry to go over the tournament particulars.

Larry was happy, the Vikings team members were overjoyed, and Principal Donna Saiki was elated—not only because her Vikings were entering the tournament, but also because of the other benefits the tournament would bring. She knew the students would benefit tremendously from the experience and that the event would strengthen the family unit. Parents, grandparents, uncles and aunties, cousins, nieces and nephews, and friends would want to attend the tournament to cheer on the Vikings.

As for the Vikings team members, none had ever been to the U.S. mainland, and Larry felt the travel would widen their horizons.

When the Hawai'i district superintendent was apprised of the tournament, however, he disapproved of the Vikings' participation.

Larry was upset. He knew that an O'ahu team had participated in a mainland tournament in the past, didn't understand why the superintendent disapproved, and he was heartbroken.

Several weeks later I ran into Principal Saiki at the Hilo post office, and I immediately apologized to her for my role in her being admonished by the district superintendent. But she shrugged off the incident and said she didn't mind being reprimanded. She strongly believed that entering the tournament would have been educational for the students. It's unfortunate the superintendent didn't feel the same.

In 2000, the Hilo High School Vikings were again crowned Big Island champions and went on to the state tournament. Just as Larry predicted, that year they were indeed crowned state champions.

Chapter 23. Harry Kim for Mayor, 2000

In election year 2000, I supported Harry Kim, a Republican candidate for mayor, along with eighteen Democratic candidates for various offices: two state senators, seven state representatives, and nine county council members.

I decided to support Harry Kim specifically because of his commitment to care for all people of this county, regardless of their income and background, and because he was my friend.

He was director of the Hawai'i County Department of Civil Defense from the late 1970s, and his office was next to mine in the former Hilo Memorial Hospital complex on Rainbow Drive. We occasionally discussed the economic, social, and political conditions of our island and the need for changes to improve the lives of all Big Islanders. I came to the conclusion that he was one of us—a product of the local culture with a good grasp of our multicultural and multiethnic society.

After Harry announced his candidacy for mayor, as a Republican, he asked me for advice. I told him that since he had limited campaign funds, he should air his campaign ads on the radio, especially in the mornings when people were driving to work and in the afternoons when they were driving home. His strength, I told him, was his voice, which was well-recognized. He had been director of Civil Defense for many years, delivering over-the-air messages of impending emergencies such as lava flows, forest fires, floods, tsunami, wind storms, and the aftermaths of earthquakes. Most Big Islanders had heard his up-to-the-minute emergency reports, as well as his reassuring "all clear" messages signifying that danger had passed, and most recognized his voice.

He was easily elected mayor of Hawai'i County, and in fact all eighteen candidates we supported won their offices.

When Harry Kim ran for a second term, it was as a Democrat and, again, he won easily.

During election years, he used to predict the winning candidate in certain races. He and I always differed, and we would place a friendly wager of one dollar on who would win. Though I never received a single dollar when he lost our wagers, Harry always supported our agency by releasing all of the program funds appropriated by the County Council.

Chapter 24. Student Success

We first hired Bernalyn Yee as a bus driver, and later she became a community facilitator of our high school dropout prevention program, where she turned out to be an exceptional worker. In her own high school days she had approached delinquency, but she somehow managed to change her attitude toward school, study hard, and receive her diploma.

When she was a community facilitator in our dropout prevention program, a school counselor assigned her twenty-five high-risk students. These were failing students who were involved in racial conflicts, exhibited antisocial behaviors, and who had an "I don't give a damn" attitude toward schoolwork, other students, and themselves.

Bernalyn had a real talent for coping with such high-risk students, individually and sometimes collectively, and for making them understand that their actions had causes and effects, both good and bad. She taught them the dos and don'ts one has to know in order to learn, as well as how to get along successfully with others. She helped students see how fighting, hating others, and neglecting studying led to regretful and unhappy outcomes.

Her efforts were amazingly successful. One year later, every single senior in the dropout prevention program received his or her high school diploma. We promoted Bernalyn to program manager and she began overseeing program activities for six high schools. They ended up with an enviable and almost unbelievable record of ninety-eight to one hundred percent of their seniors receiving high school diplomas!

Perhaps, I always thought, part of the program's success came from our staff members being considered understanding second parents to the students, many of whom came from broken families that didn't provide parental affection and guidance.

Rose Kuamoʻo was another exceptional community facilitator of our dropout prevention program. She was assigned to Hilo High School. At a program staff meeting, Rose mentioned that many of her clients, who were from poor families, wanted to pursue higher education, especially learning a trade at the community college, but their families could not afford to send them.

> Rose Kuamoʻo later left us to work for Alu Like, an organization serving native Hawaiians.

I replied that there was a way for students to learn a trade and even get paid to do it. The solution, I proposed, was for them to enlist in the U.S. Armed Forces, such as the peacetime U.S. Army. The Army had changed, I explained, and become more modernized. Enlisted men and women now received technical training in electronics, mechanics, and many other trades. And, above all, they got paid. They were fed three meals a day, and had a career path laid out for them with numerous benefits, including retirement at an earlier age than was available to civilians.

Rose contacted the local Army recruitment office and invited its recruitment sergeant to speak to her student-clients. He came and explained eligibility requirements. The most important requirements, he said, were to pass both a written test and a physical examination. Inspired, the students pursued their academic work with new vigor. After graduating from high school in 2000, nineteen students enlisted in the Army.

Terror and War, 2001

And then, calamity struck.

On September 11, 2001, New York City's Twin Towers were destroyed by terrorists, and more than four thousand civilians were killed. Soon afterward, America was at war. Those nineteen enlisted Hilo men were all sent to fight in Iraq.

I was so worried for their safety and prayed often for their safe return. It was an absolute miracle that all nineteen of them eventually returned home safe and sound. I felt a tremendous sense of relief after having been the one to suggest they enlist in the Army. The soldiers' first order of business was to see Rose, their surrogate parent. It must have made Rose extremely happy that those boys remembered her. Many of them remained in the Army and pursued a career path.

Though the September 11 crisis was far away, it created a ripple effect like a tidal wave roaring onto our Island shores. Hawai'i state depends on the tourist industry for sustainability—and unexpectedly, abruptly, the visitors stopped arriving. Tour buses stopped operating and almost no tourists visited Rainbow Falls, where, nearby, our income-producing projects were waiting for them.

By November, we had closed our Open Market and gift shop and curtailed our confectionary gift production. Although visitors slowly began trickling back to Rainbow Falls, their numbers were way too small to sustain our income-producing projects, which were essentially wiped out.

We took solace, though, in knowing we had helped approximately nine hundred and fifty economically disadvantaged individuals by giving them job training and placement and by helping them change their attitudes toward work, family, and community. We'd given almost a thousand people a new perspective on life.

Chapter 25. Governorship, 2002

In the 2002 gubernatorial election, Lieutenant Governor Mazie Hirono and State Representative Ed Case competed against each other in the Democratic primary, and both were notable candidates. In the Republican primary election, Governor Linda Lingle was being thought of as a shoo-in, meaning that her campaign war chest could be saved for the main event—the general election.

I was inundated with requests for support from both the Hirono and Case camps, and I carefully considered which candidate had the best chance of challenging Lingle in the general election.

I had never spoken with Hirono before, although I'd had brief, sporadic encounters with her, specifically in hearings of the House Committee on Consumer Affairs, of which she was a member. A lifeline bill for low-income seniors to receive electricity discounts had died in that committee. She was of Japanese descent, and in the general election she would most likely win the Japanese votes, I predicted, but lose among other ethnic groups, particularly among haole voters.

Whereas, I pondered, if Case—whom I had never met or spoken to—was up against Lingle in the general election, he would probably receive about the same number of Japanese votes, as Japanese voters usually vote for the Democratic candidate. He would also likely amass votes from other ethnic groups.

Matt Matsunaga, son of the late U.S. Senator Spark Matsunaga, was a candidate for lieutenant governor and he was leading in the polls. A Hirono/Matsunaga combination of two Japanese for top state leadership was not as strong as the Case/Matsunaga combination, I decided, when competing against Lingle/Aiona.

If past patterns held true, Lieutenant Governor Hirono would become governor, because in the past, Lieutenant Governors Ariyoshi, Waihee and Cayetano had all succeeded in becoming governor. But a fortnight's consideration made me believe that Lieutenant Governor Hirono's chances to win in the general election were very slim.

I remembered an incident that happened when Linda Lingle was mayor of Maui County and I used that to my advantage. Gladys Baisa, the politically savvy executive director of Maui Economic Opportunity, told me that Mayor Lingle had approved an appreciable amount of funding for her transportation program and really cared about the economically disadvantaged people of Maui. Mayor Lingle was a guest speaker at a Hawai'i County Council meeting at about the time I was advocating for direly needed transportation program funds, and I thought of a subtle way to better our chances of increasing our own transportation funds.

During Mayor Lingle's speech, I hastily jotted down a question for her and handed it to councilwoman Bobby Jean Leithead-Todd. During the Q&A session, Bobby Jean asked the mayor my question: How much did Maui County Economic Opportunity receive for its transportation program?

"Six million dollars," replied Lingle. She explained that she was committed to serving the disadvantaged people of Maui County with fairness to all the poor, elderly, and the disabled, which included providing mobility to medical facilities and other public and private service institutions such as banks, the Social Security office, post office, and shopping. She sounded like a Democrat.

When she finished her response, I stood up and walked to the council room door where I turned around, faced our council members, and saluted them. The nine council members smiled and nodded as if acknowledging my plea to increase our transportation funding. I waved my hand to them in appreciation, and walked out of the council room feeling very satisfied.

When the council made its funding decisions, they unanimously, without quibbling, approved our request to increase our transportation program funds to $600,000. It was a paltry amount compared to Maui's six million dollars, but it was the best our county could manage during its economic depression.

Lingle as a Strong Contender

Linda Lingle was a formidable Republican candidate. In the previous general election, against Ben Cayetano, she had won the Democratic stronghold of the Big Island by more than five thousand votes. Fortunately, Cayetano had won Oʻahu by more than five thousand votes and he had retained his governorship by a squeaker.

For me, this election was going to be predicated upon who had a better chance of winning, not on who was most qualified to be our next governor. If someone supports us, we offer our support. That's my method. Even if they're a Republican, like Richard Henderson. We supported him because he supported us. The same with Virginia Isbell. No second guessing. I learned my lesson with Dante Carpenter. We supported him in the first election and then he slashed the most critical program for the seniors. The council put it back 9–0. Then 9–0 the next year, and 9–0 the next year. Zero zero zero. He must be embarrassed.

Ed Case was labeled by the union as being against the working people. But I decided to support Ed Case for governor and Matt Matsunaga for lieutenant governor, and this caused a rush of anger among many of my friends and fellow past campaigners. Some thought I was being presumptuous, arrogant, and had become a wheeler-dealer. They thought I was overstepping my usual boundaries of grassroots campaigning for the candidate who best advocated for the well-being of the poor, but I just ignored them. We were usually pretty quiet, but sometimes things just aren't right and you have to make them known. I talked to our people and we did what we thought was best.

In the primary election, Hirono won the Big Island by a margin of 1.4 percent, and statewide she nosed out Case by less than one percent. Matt Matsunaga won the lieutenant governor's primary race. It was, therefore, the Hirono/Matsunaga ballot that went on to challenge Lingle and Aiona in the general election.

As I predicted, Lingle and Aiona won the election. Linda Lingle became only the second Republican governor of Hawaiʻi since statehood in 1959.

I was satisfied that all the candidates we supported for other county and state races won, but I felt insecure about the new Republican administration. I didn't know if Governor Lingle would follow the conservative direction of President Bush, who zeroed out Community Service Block Grant (CSBG) funds of $700 million from his presidential budget when he submitted it to Congress. That affected more than one thousand community action agencies. Every Republican president from Nixon on zeroed out CSBG, except for President Ford.

Every single time, however, Congress reinstated and appropriated CSBG funds in order to sustain community action agencies. This was with the support of Democrats, Republicans, and Independents, and with the tireless and effective advocacy efforts of David Bradley, the executive director of the National Community Action Foundation.

On the home front, I was worried that we might not receive state program funds from a Republican administration, and I sought advice from State Representative Dwight Takamine, chair of the House Committee on Finance. He recommended that I submit our grant applications as usual. He reminded me that state statutes allow grants to non-profit organizations for public purposes; that grants are appropriated by the state legislature, forwarded to the governor for approval, and then released to the applicants by the governor; and that the governor, however, had the discretion to restrict or not release grant funds for "justifiable reasons."

He felt that it was a good time to "test the waters," so I immediately prepared seven grant applications for programs to continue serving the needy: ten twenty-one-passenger buses for transportation for the elderly, disabled, and low-income preschool children; our Language Arts Multicultural Program (LAMP); our high school dropout prevention program; agricultural training; renewable energy training program; employment core services; and our incubation kitchen for value-added products programs.

In January of 2003, we submitted the grant applications to the state legislature. Appropriations were expected to be made in May. We received $600,000 for the purchase of the buses in the first year, then $1.2 million per year, for each of two years, to be divided between the other six programs.

In the meanwhile, Governor Lingle replaced the heads of state departments, agencies, and offices with Republicans. Sam Aiona, former state representative, former chair of the state Republican party, and first cousin to Lieutenant Governor James Aiona, was appointed executive director of the state Office of Community Services (OCS) to oversee the four community action agencies of Kauaʻi, Oʻahu, Maui, and Hawaiʻi for the implementation of the CSBG state plan. OCS was attached to the state Department of Labor and Industrial Relations for administrative purposes, with the responsibility of allocating federal CSBG and state funds and monitoring operations of the four agencies.

Sam came to Hilo for a courtesy visit and to be oriented on our programs, and it was a nice visit. He told me he had been born and raised in Hilo, attended St. Joseph School from kindergarten to twelfth grade, and that he had been on St. Joseph's high school basketball team.

I called our deputy director Larry Manliguis and asked him to come to my office. Larry, who was still a part-time coach for the Hilo High School Vikings basketball team, recognized Sam as a star player whose team, the Cardinals, had played against the Vikings. They chatted about basketball and reminisced about winning and losing certain hard-fought games.

I also called our LAMP manager Sharon Sakoda, who recognized Sam at once when she entered my office. He had been her student at St. Joseph, and they had a wonderful reunion, too. By the time Sharon and Larry left, congeniality had been well-established. Sam and I discussed our program to his satisfaction, and then the conversation switched to politics.

I knew Sam had been elected to the state House of Representatives but then lost in a subsequent bid for re-election. His chairing the state Republican party made me realize he was a politician at heart, but whether he was one who was involved in party politics for personal gain or other selfish interests, I did not know.

He extolled the virtues of Governor Lingle, saying she cared about the economically disadvantaged, and he extolled her accomplishments as two-term mayor of Maui County, particularly her having funded programs for the poor through Maui Economic Opportunity.

I surmised that at this still-early stage, Sam was already preparing for Lingle's 2006 gubernatorial election. He knew that I had the support of grassroots campaigners, and in a dignified manner he told me that he would like to arrange an introductory meeting between Governor Lingle and me. I accepted the invitation, aware that our grant applications would ultimately arrive at her desk and require her approval and release of funds.

On the appointed date and time, I went to the fifth floor of the state Capitol building and found Sam waiting for me at the entrance to the governor's office. Unfortunately, the governor had to attend an emergency meeting and was not in, but she had left instructions to introduce me to Chief of Staff Bob Awana, who greeted me by saying, "I've heard a lot about you." He told Sam to introduce me to Linda Smith, senior policy advisor to the governor. Sam escorted me to her office and left after introducing us.

My meeting with Linda Smith was courteous and cordial. She told me that as senior policy advisor, her duties were to advise the governor on policy decisions regarding matters that came to her desk, both monetary and non-monetary ones, including grants and subsidies to organizations.

She asked me about the work I did and the programs we operated, and I told her about socioeconomic conditions in Hawai'i County. I told her about the problems and needs of welfare and food stamp recipients, which were the highest in the state, as well as unemployment rates, and the lack of industry development to take the place of the sugar industry that had recently ended after more than a century. I said all contributed to crime, alcoholism, suicides, school dropouts, juvenile delinquency, and an increasing low-income population that included the elderly. Finally, I told her that the Big Island had the distinction of having the state's lowest per capita income. It was because of these dire conditions and needs that we established our programs, I explained.

Our conversation was non-political and lasted for more than an hour. She adhered to the protocol of a senior policy adviser and never mentioned, nor solicited, anything of a political nature. I did not ask for her support in having the governor release our funds, should they be appropriated. Yet I was very satisfied to have the chance to convey the Big Island's problems and needs, and I hoped I had swayed Linda Smith to give favorable advice to the governor when our grant applications were considered.

Near the end of May, the legislature appropriated all of our grant funds for the biennial fiscal year that started July 1, 2003, and ended June 30, 2005. To our great relief and joy, Governor Lingle released all of our grant funds.

Success Stories

Ann Matson was a community facilitator we assigned to Waiākea High School. She was a thoughtful and caring individual, mature in her ability to assess problem students and find positive ways to place them on track for their overall intellectual development. One of those "problem students" was the aforementioned Jessica Yamamoto, who later became an employee. As a teenager, Jessica's behaviors were far from the norm, and she was off track from her peers.

When she was fifteen-and-a-half years old, Jessica was kicked out of her home for defiance and revolting against her parents, and had to fend for herself. She found a job at Sure Save Supermarket. Ann Matson took Jessica under her wing, nurtured her to get her on the right track, and cared for her until she graduated from high school. Recognizing that Jessica had the potential to be successful, Ann persuaded her to pursue higher education. Jessica enrolled at the University of Hawai'i at Mānoa, and went on to graduate with a 3.85 grade point average.

When she returned to Hilo, we hired her to establish a computer learning center where low-income individuals could enhance their employment opportunities. Computer skills were becoming very important because employers were starting to prefer computer-literate individuals, even for clerical positions.

As the computer learning center's manager, Jessica designed a curriculum that fit the needs of local low-income individuals. With a three-year federal grant, the center was able to train many low-income mothers. It was encouraging and heartwarming to see mothers working on the computer with a crib set up right next to them.

Our computer learning center graduates had tremendous advantages over other job seekers. Forty-six students were hired for permanent positions.

Next, Jessica Yamamoto managed the high school dropout prevention program. Because she'd been a client during her own high school years, she understood the need and urgency for our program to help potential dropouts stay on the right track.

When Larry Manliguis passed away in 2007, she was promoted to deputy director for community services. Later she earned her master's degree, and got a job at the University of Hawai'i at Hilo and then at

Hawai'i Community College. She reconciled with her father, a skilled carpenter, who built her a house in the Puna district.

Unfortunately for us, Jessica Yamamoto left our agency to take a higher position and better pay with the state government, but I was consoled by the fact that she succeeded in lifting herself to a higher standard in life.

I needed a replacement, and hoped to find someone of the same demeanor and caliber as Jessica. Alda Gomes was a part-time accountant in our fiscal office, attended Hawai'i Community College, and I found her to be intelligent, persistent, and motivated. I placed an in-house announcement of the executive secretary position, Alda applied, and we hired her.

Her administrative duties included preparing reports, taking committee and board meeting minutes, and gathering data on needs and problems in our community as a basis for our grant application requests. I sent her to a grant writing seminar, and she became an important part of our grant writing team; many times she worked around the clock until the sun came up again in the morning.

Chapter 26. More Funding

From 2003 to 2008, encouraged by our success at obtaining county and state level grants, we again turned to the federal government. We submitted applications for four three-year grants, at two-year intervals, and all four were funded.

One was for a biotech tissue culture project that would establish a tissue culture laboratory for cloning ornamental orchid plants, and another was to expand that project to include the cloning of other exotic ornamental plants, specifically vanilla and green tea. The third was for the cultivation of *Jatropha curcas* seeds for biofuel production. Those grants averaged $700,000 and we had an additional $400,000 in non-federal contributions from the state government, for a total of $1.1 million per project.

The projects were headed by Robert Burkey, an exceptionally capable individual who enlisted the support of Dr. Kheng Cheah, an expert on plant tissue culture and transgenic plant production. At the onset of the project, Dr. Cheah conducted classes on plant tissue culture and other requirements of laboratory work for low-income welfare clients. Since she lived in Honolulu and could not conduct daily classes, Bob Burkey assumed the bulk of the daily work—from the technical aspects of laboratory work to how to build a team of qualified laboratory technicians, including how to encourage motivation and persistence so technicians become economically self-sufficient.

It was especially significant that, in a short period, trainees learned not only the skills required for tissue culture work, but also how to explain the details of plant cloning and other tissue culture work to visitors. The visitors, many of them in the plant nursery business, were amazed at the professionalism our trainees exhibited, and were further astonished to later discover that many were single-parent welfare recipients learning a trade.

The fourth grant, for a renewable energy project, was for $680,000, and we had some non-federal contributions of about $400,000 from the state government. This project was headed by Dr. Max Goldberger.

The aim of all four projects was to create jobs for capable welfare recipients who would undergo training and then be placed in the relatively new and growing industries.

Non-federal dollar contributions to all four projects were from the state Department of Human Services (DHS) and from the state Office of Community Services, and were used as stipends for TANF clients.

For twenty-four consecutive years, we were fortunate to receive non-federal monetary support from the directors of DHS, starting with Winona Rubin under Governor Waihee, Susan Chandler under Governor Cayetano, and Lillian Koller under Governor Lingle.

In 2005, we again submitted our state grant applications for the biennium with a total request of $1.5 million. That included $380,000 for the Right Track Program, a new drug abuse prevention program for high-risk high school students.

It made use of funding made possible by the 2003–2004 joint House-Senate task force on ice (methamphetamine) and drug abatement, which was co-chaired by Representative Eric Hamakawa and Senator Colleen Hanabusa.

It was very fortunate we had supported Representative Hamakawa in his successful run for the state House of Representatives; we had also befriended his father, Kiyo, a retired Hilo High School vice principal, when advocating for funds for our high school dropout prevention program. And although Senator Hanabusa represented Oʻahu, we had become very good friends, to the extent that I could walk into her office without a prior appointment.

The task force conducted statewide public hearings on ice and drug abatement, and we had been present at all the Big Island hearings to ensure that our group was represented, with testifiers making a pitch for our program. It was after that, in 2005, that the legislative agenda included an invitation to bid for program funds. We did so and were successful.

Voices

I was at the state Capitol, attending those 2005 legislative hearings, and people had gathered around the entrance to the public hearing rooms in two clusters, waiting for the doors to open.

As I walked past the first hearing room, heading for the Committee on Finance hearing, I heard someone call my name.

"George Yokoyama!"

It was a familiar voice, one often heard on television and radio, and in a split-second glance out of the corner of my eye, I recognized the tall, slim figure. It was Governor Linda Lingle.

I continued walking past the crowd as if nothing had happened, but I was dumbfounded that she knew me. I'd never been introduced to her, nor spoken with her. I was just shocked that she knew me, and I didn't want to talk to her in front of everyone, because she was a Republican. I felt good, though, surmising that the governor must have learned my name from her senior policy adviser Linda Smith. Or perhaps she'd come across my name during the previous biennium, while signing documents to release funds to our agency, which meant she knew me through the programs we operated for the economically disadvantaged. But that did not explain how she recognized me in person.

The Committee on Finance approved our grant requests and referred them to the Senate Committee on Ways and Means. Finally, the state legislature appropriated the funds for our programs and Governor Lingle released them, although because of the state's budget crunch she released some of them belatedly.

On the county government level, it became an annual ritual for us to advocate for county funds for our transportation program at the county council budget hearing. The hearing room would be packed with our clients, who were elderly people and disabled citizens in wheelchairs.

There were some skirmishes during the hearings. A newly elected council member asked why our transportation program duplicated services provided by the county's mass transit system. I explained that mass transit bus stops are on the highway, whereas many of our clients lived on narrow roads in former plantation camps that were two to three miles away from the highway. Therefore, walking to a bus stop becomes a tremendous burden for elderly people, and out of the question for disabled people in wheelchairs. I emphasized that our transportation provided a human service and not a mass transit type of service, and therefore we did not duplicate services.

Someone asked who paid to transport clients to county budget hearings and using what funds, implying that it was a questionably allowable activity of our agency. I responded that we used Community Services Block Grant (CSBG) funds, and that the CSBG plan calls for the poor to have the maximum feasible participation in community affairs that affect their lives. I stated that a critical need for transportation was indeed a community affair that affected their lives, and therefore it was an allowable activity of the CSBG plan.

The council voted 9–0 to approve our transportation funds, and Mayor Harry Kim released the funds to us without hesitation.

Chapter 27. Elections of 2006

Sam Aiona, director of the state Office of Community Services (OCS), treated me like a VIP and tried to persuade me to support Governor Linda Lingle for her second term of office, but I had to politely decline. I told him that although Governor Lingle had demonstrated her commitment to supporting programs for the disadvantaged, I had a higher calling—U.S. Senator Daniel Akaka needed my help.

Congressman Ed Case had announced his candidacy for U.S. Senator, running against Dan Akaka. Ed was a freshman congressman who had served only one term in Congress, but he had the audacity to challenge the incumbent Dan Akaka for the Senate seat and, furthermore, to suggest that Akaka was too old for the job! I told Sam that I had to concentrate our grassroots efforts exclusively on Dan Akaka, as I had supported him throughout the years since 1976 and he needed my help. I was fulfilling my obligation to him after all his years of support for CSBG and our other needs in Washington relative to our community action programs.

I contacted Roland Higashi, who was managing the Ed Case campaign. We had been on the same team, campaigning for gubernatorial candidates George Ariyoshi, John Waihee, and Ben Cayetano, as well as mayoral candidate Steven Yamashiro; all were successful two-term candidates with the exception of Ariyoshi, who served three terms. I told Roland to choose his weapon. It became a duel between Roland and me, but a friendly one.

Richard Onishi, who was coordinating Dan Akaka's campaign on the Big Island, asked me to help him in the outlying districts. We concentrated our campaign efforts in Puna, Volcano, Kaʻū, North and South

Kona, Waimea, Kohala, Hāmākua, North Hilo and, in Hilo, the Keaukaha and Panaʻewa precincts, which are Hawaiian Home Lands, where a majority of the residents are Native Hawaiians.

Other individuals came to lend a helping hand with our grassroots efforts, as well. State Representative Dwight Takamine was instrumental in organizing a fundraiser for Akaka at the Civic Auditorium, Larry Mehau sponsored a gathering at his Waimea ranch, and Rockne Freitas mobilized fifty volunteer workers for a Hawaiian lūʻau gathering at Aunty Sally's Lūʻau Hale, with guest speakers Donn Ariyoshi and Reverend Tuck Wah Lee.

Dan Akaka won the primary, and then easily won the general election. And Governor Lingle won her second term of office.

I expressed my personal gratitude to Harold Bugado, Larry Manliguis, and George Hanohano after each campaign since 1974. I thanked them for their tireless efforts helping candidates who supported our cause of uplifting the poor, which they did by becoming the primary leaders of our grassroots campaign's community core groups. They participated in countless community campaign meetings, house-to-house canvassing, manning campaign booths at the County Fair, sign-waving, person-to-person contacts, and other chores of campaigning.

In 2007, the nation's approaching recession began affecting Hawaiʻi, and by 2009, the state government was in bad financial straits. Governor Lingle instituted weekly furlough Fridays, on which state government workers and later county workers were required to take an unpaid leave. This somewhat eased the financial burden on both state and county governments.

Hawaii State Governors

1974 Ariyoshi
1978 Ariyoshi
1982 Ariyoshi
1986 Waihee
1990 Waihee
1994 Cayetano
1998 Cayetano
2002 Lingle
2006 Lingle
2010 Abercrombie
2014 Ige

And then that same year, Representative Dwight Takamine, the powerful chair of the Committee on Finance and our crucial link to grant funding, was ousted. This came about after an unfounded impression that he had intruded on the prerogatives of the House Speaker during an attempted House leadership shake-up by dissident Democrats. In actuality, Dwight had been asked by U.S. Senator Daniel Inouye to mediate between the opposing Democratic factions.

Our relationship with the House Committee on Finance was weaker after Dwight left, but we were able to solicit the support of the new chair of the House Finance Committee, Representative Marcus Oshiro. We did this through my long-time friend Mike Amii, who was the reliable right hand of Marcus's father Bob Oshiro, who had led many gubernatorial campaigns. I also gained the support of Senate President Colleen Hanabusa and Senate Vice President Russell Kokubun.

Despite the state budget crunch, we were fortunate and successful in receiving our share of grant funds and grateful to Governor Lingle for releasing those funds to us; although they were delayed, we received them in adequate time.

In the 2008 political elections, we supported Billy Kenoi for mayor and Representative Takamine for state senator, along with the usual county council members and state legislators who were supportive of our programs. All were elected.

Billy Kenoi is a product of the Big Island, born in Kalapana and educated with an attorney's degree. He served as a staff member at the state Office of Community Services and was familiar with the missions of community action agencies. It was my natural tendency to support him for mayor of our county.

But more than that, Billy proved to be a polished speaker and a positive thinker with wisdom, wit, and humor in presenting the needs and solutions to our county's problems in conversations and speeches that moved whomever he needed to convince. He was a local, polished, and congenial Hawaiian with the knack of switching easily from Pidgin to standard English as the situation required and was able to easily propose solutions and reach consensus on problems.

Billy supported us even before he became mayor. He testified for us at county council hearings on our budget requests for our transportation program. I joined Roland Higashi in Billy's campaign for mayor and Billy won easily.

Chapter 28. Conniving at Head Start

In 2008, our Head Start program director, Diana Kahler, retired after many years of service and an enviable record of accomplishments. She stayed on and continued to serve until we could find her replacement, which was a difficult endeavor since no one locally seemed to qualify—we had to advertise nationally. The regional office kept calling me to expedite filling the position. Finally some applications came in, and our Head Start policy council screened and interviewed them. It recommended the top candidates in order of first to third choices.

I hired their first choice, and it turned out to be one of the biggest mistakes I ever made.

During the new director's first six months, which was her probationary period, she performed well and adhered to the protocol of a superior-subordinate relationship. However, once she became a permanent employee, her behavior changed drastically.

Trouble

The new Head Start director frequently called the regional office in San Francisco, which was a clear violation of the chain of command. When she wanted something done that I didn't agree with, she just called there; then the regional office called and instructed me to do what she wanted done, as if the instruction came directly from them.

The program's senior manager cautioned me that the new director was plotting to oust me, so she could become executive director herself. She confided in me, saying that the Head Start director belittled me by saying that running an organization the size of ours was beyond the experience of a local person, and in order for our agency to excel, it needed a new executive director with U.S. mainland experience.

It became clear that her style of managing personnel by fear, intimidation, and connivance was becoming the norm. Within a short time, she became an insider informant to the regional office, informing them of my apparent infractions of the rules.

What I learned from the experience was that we had to be so careful about bringing in managers from the mainland. Some don't understand the culture here and have totally different ways of thinking. Some seem to think we're all Neanderthals who don't know anything.

The director's most outrageous act was returning more than $260,000 in unexpended funds to the regional Head Start office without my knowledge or permission. This was unlike Diana Kahler, who worked with me to reallocate unused funds for program supplies and to increase the allocation of percentage work time of fiscal officers, accountants, bookkeepers, and other administrative staff commensurate with the workload increase in closing out the Head Start program fiscal year.

Most of the unexpended funds were created by a large turnover of Head Start program staff, many of whom left because of low morale. Replacing them took two or three months, which created an unusual amount of funds due to unexpended salaries.

It was such a mess. I was being bombarded from within the ranks. Everything was bypassing me and going to the regional Head Start office, and the word was all derogatory. There was a big push to get me out as director.

The regional office sent a representative to conduct a cursory inspection of our agency, followed by a team of regional officials for in-depth monitoring and evaluation of our program. It resulted in a scathing report listing discrepancies in our Head Start program as well as the following pronouncement: Termination of the Head Start program, in which case a program closeout team would be dispatched to the agency, or, in the event of voluntary relinquishment of the program, a transitional team would be sent to transfer the program to another entity operating child development programs at a lower cost.

This was all happening at a time when the federal government, due to the national economic depression, was on an economy drive to reduce federal spending, and our program was seemingly targeted for reduction in funding or defunding.

Harold Bugado, chair of our board, convened a board meeting. After he consulted with the members, and with the assurance that the Head Start program would continue under a new entity, we voted to voluntarily relinquish administration of the program.

The regional office chose Parents and Children Together (PACT), which was based on the island of Oʻahu, to take over Head Start. My good friend was the executive there at PACT, and I put in a good word for them to get it. They did. Although it was a small organization, PACT was acceptable to administer the program because it operated a Head Start program on Oʻahu and was very well versed in the program's administration. PACT was a single purpose organization, formed solely to operate Head Start. The regional office's decision to select PACT to take over Head Start was a reasonable one; it reduced administrative overhead costs and PACT was able to operate the program with experienced staff who were carried over from our agency to theirs.

I knew the PACT people and I knew they would do a good job, so I just let it go. And the woman who caused all the trouble got fired. But the regional office really meddled that time. There was a drive to take out bad Head Start programs in order to save money, and we became a target.

Repulsive Consequences of Living by the Political Sword

In early 2009, people were already talking about the next year's gubernatorial election and posing a lot of questions. Would a Republican again be elected as governor? Or was Linda Lingle merely an accidental governor—would state leadership again revert to a Democratic governor?

There were Republicans, and others in high, appointed state government positions, who had a comfortable income and wanted it to continue. They started to get serious about preparing for the next election by laying the groundwork, especially to accentuate the positive and eliminate the negatives in the early campaign stages.

Several Republicans called and tried to persuade me to support lieutenant governor James Aiona for governor. He had roots and many relatives in Hilo, including his first cousin Sam Aiona. But I politely declined. I called Sam, who had recently served as chair of the state Republican party, to be apprised of the political pulse on the Republican side.

Sam said that everyone in the political circle knew me as one of the movers and shakers in politics, and remembered the *Honolulu Advertiser* article published years ago that said just that. Surprisingly, though, he did not try to persuade me to support his cousin James, perhaps knowing that I would decline. My relationship with Sam was always an amicable one.

Nonetheless, word went around that I would be a hindrance to a Republican candidate, whomever it was, and that I should be ousted from my position because of my grassroots power that consistently resulted in campaign victories—the people I campaigned for won.

Politics had finally merged with community action programs. It turned out there was a vicious, multi-pronged attack from both within and without. All had the same objective—my ouster—but for distinctly different reasons.

It started in early 2009, when a recently hired program specialist in charge of the state's CSBG programs paid a courtesy visit to our agency. She wanted an orientation of the programs we operated. She introduced herself as having a law degree and spoke as though she were an authority on the state CSBG plan. I wondered why an individual with a law degree would work for such a moderate Office of Community Services salary.

First she asked me whether or not our agency had a board of directors manual. I told her, "No," and she adamantly insisted that I prepare one. I politely asked her for the regulation that stated we were required to have a board manual, and she could not answer me, but still insisted that I prepare one. I told her that I had reviewed several board manuals, some of them three inches thick, and that my board and I had decided that our agency bylaws were enough. They spelled out everything—the purpose, mission, and responsibilities, including committee function and procedures, for our board members to follow.

Moreover, I told her, our tripartite board of public, private, and low-income sectors undergo board training and were well-versed in board functions. I emphasized that our board members were unpaid volunteers, and the low-income board members with educations of high school or less would have a difficult time with a thick, rigid manual.

As she left, though, she again insisted that I prepare a board manual. I knew they were plotting to get me out any way they could. The best way they thought was to evaluate our program and give a terrible report.

I called Sam Aiona and told him I had talked to my lawyer and had every right to file a suit against her.

She returned in the second week of March to conduct a two-day monitoring and evaluation of our agency, and this time her visit was official business. Her title had changed to CSBG administrator, and I realized that Sam had promoted her and deferred to her, and that, due to her background as an attorney, he relied on her legal advice regarding matters pertaining to CSBG programs.

In April, we received the results of her monitoring. To me, the report seemed full of innuendos and lacked supporting evidence. These people come here thinking they know everything, but they don't know anything. She sent a copy of the report to Darwin Ching, state director of Labor and Industrial Relations and then we had a telephone conference call. I was on one end of the line, and Darwin Ching, Sam Aiona, and the CSBG administrator were on the other.

Darwin Ching started by saying the governor had given him full authority to oversee disbursement of President Obama's American Recovery and Reinvestment Act (ARRA) funds to Hawai'i's community action agencies. Nearly a million dollars of that funding was earmarked for our agency that year. Because of the findings in the monitoring report, though, and unless we corrected the deficiencies, he said he could not recommend the governor release the funds. I told Darwin Ching we would do our best to correct them.

Immediately after the conference call, I sent Sam Aiona a rebuttal of the monitoring report. I emphasized that the report contained allegations without any supporting evidence. I had shown an attorney friend the monitoring report, and he told me it contained frivolous accusations, lacked evidence, and would not hold up in a court of law. He volunteered to represent us in court if I decided to file a legal complaint.

In the meantime, the CSBG administrator brought in a program monitoring and evaluation team to evaluate the state's four community action agencies. I spoke to a reliable friend in Washington, D.C., who was highly versed on consultant firms doing business with community action agencies throughout the nation. His advice to me?

"George, don't ever hire that company," he said firmly. They'd defunded a couple community action agencies. Times were hard and the CSBG had called the company to shut them down, he told me.

I went online to read more about that company's background and learned quite a bit. One community action agency was defunded as a result of its evaluation report; several others were on the verge of becoming high-risk agencies.

The CSBG administrator had contracts with that company covering all community action agencies in Hawaiʻi. I challenged that, saying our fiscal policy stipulated that expenditures over $5,000 must be put out to at least three contractors for bidding. I questioned, too, whether the company the CSBG had a contract with was licensed to do business in the state of Hawaiʻi.

But Sam told me that unless I signed the contract with that company, we would not receive the ARRA funds. I reluctantly signed the contract, which was for nearly $50,000 and included services for staff training.

A team of evaluators arrived at our agency, and we held a board meeting to be oriented as to what monitoring activities would occur over the next five days. They told us that at 6 p.m. on Friday, they would present the results of the monitoring to our board of directors. Each board member would receive a copy of the report.

The CEO introduced herself at the board meeting, followed by the company's chief financial officer and other team members. Monitoring procedures were explained, and then monitoring began the next morning. The CEO interviewed me in a rather cursory way, with standard questions on staff organization, personnel, administration, planning, and program implementation.

My interview with the CFO, though, was much more detailed. It concerned whether or not we were keeping accurate income and expenditure records, our overall financial planning, the maintenance of our financial records, and the preparation and submission of fiscal reports to funding sources.

I responded to all his questions, starting with the procedure for proper accounting of expenditures for each of the eighteen programs we operated at that time (we kept separate files for each program account). I explained how we purchased program supplies and equipment using a one-page requisition form that was signed by the requisitioner, the program supervisor, and the division director and then forwarded to the fiscal office, whereupon the pre-audit clerk reviewed the requisition for accuracy and justification of the purchase prior to issuing and recording a purchase order number; it was submitted to the fiscal officer for fiscal review and approval, and then sent to the executive director for final approval and signature. I told the CFO I did not sign any requisition without the assigned purchase order number and the specific program to be charged.

For monthly fiscal reports, I told him, the fiscal officer compiled expenditures of each of the eighteen programs, in order to ascertain that all funds were expended properly and without excessive over- or underspending. We distributed copies of these fiscal reports at our monthly board of directors' meetings for review and approval. In addition, we used monthly reports to complete and submit financial reports to funding sources on a semi-annual basis. At no point during or after our interview did the CFO raise questions of impropriety regarding our fiscal procedures.

Our agency's monitoring and evaluation was completed, and we held a special board meeting on Friday evening. Sam Aiona and Darwin Ching came to my office about two hours before the board meeting, which they would attend.

Darwin introduced himself and reiterated that the governor had asked him to oversee the ARRA funds. He talked about being accustomed to coming to Hilo. His daughter lived in Hilo and worked for Jay Kimura, the county prosecutor who was also a board member of HCEOC. He had many friends in Hilo, he told me.

And then, abruptly, he asked, "When are you going to step down?"

"I never thought of stepping down," I replied.

Why were they trying to get rid of me? They knew that the candidates I supported won. Starting with Akaka, I brought the ones that were going to lose back up. I was a serious threat.

Former Senator Andrew Levin had become chief of staff for Harry Kim, and he, too, had an agenda. Both Andy and Harry were out of jobs in January, and Andy had the idea he would kick me out and move Harry into my job at HCEOC. I can prove that. I have the email.

I told my good friend, the attorney Sandy Song, "Over my dead body."

I told her, "I won't leave. I'll step down from the position because of the $1 million, but I'm staying." I did end up stepping down from being executive director of HCEOC in 2009, but they wanted me out of there completely. Nope.

Findings

At the board meeting, the CEO presented her company's findings and its recommendations for corrective actions. Among the substantive recommendations were to decrease the board's membership size, rewrite our bylaws, and phase out unprofitable income-producing projects. Finally, in an earnest voice, the CEO suggested our agency "prohibit the executive director from making future program or financial commitments for the organization without reviews by the fiscal officer and approval by the governing board."

I was stunned by her comments, especially the remark, "Prohibit the executive director from making future program or financial commitments." That shocked me because for each program we operated, we were bound by approved budgets and programmatic interventions for which our grant was awarded. Any deviations from the grant contract required prior approval from the funding source, along with the concurrence of our fiscal office and the whole board. Her statement represented an entirely different view from that of the chief financial officer who had interviewed me.

The CEO commented on our HCEOC employees, too, saying they did not seriously adhere to required tasks and showed little concern for some matters. As an example, she said that she had instructed our executive secretary to inform the state CSBG administrator that a certain task needed to be done by a certain date but that the CSBG administrator never received the message. Our employees lacked a sense of responsibility, she concluded.

However, she gave her orders to that executive secretary during a meeting and they had been recorded on audiotape. That tape proved that it was the CEO's error, not our employee's.

It was not a carefully prepared, accurate report.

Andy Levin, our agency's interim board chair, came to my office the next morning. He had talked with Darwin Ching the evening before, he said, after the board's assessment meeting and before Darwin returned to Honolulu. He was cordial but implored me to step down from my executive director position, or else we would lose the direly needed ARRA funds. He explained he was not asking me to resign, but to voluntarily step down and take another position within HCEOC. He said that our bylaws stipulated that two-thirds of the board had to vote to terminate the executive director, but of our twenty-seven board members, he had only three confirmed votes.

I agreed to step down in order to preserve the important ARRA funds. He suggested that I recommend, in writing to the executive committee, that they create a position appropriate for me. I drafted a proposal to create a new position for resource mobilization through advocacy and grant writing. I told him I would be very comfortable with this position, as I had been mobilizing funds for the agency for more than thirty-eight years, as an extra job, mostly on my own time and in addition to my primary duties of running the agency. He agreed.

However, when he called the executive committee meeting to order, he hesitated. He had a change of heart about the board creating a new position for me and did not present my written proposal.

A few days later, at another executive committee meeting, he came up with an alternate proposal: hiring former mayor Harry Kim, who had been unemployed since January 2009, as interim executive director. Andy himself, formerly chief-of-staff under Mayor Kim, had fortunately found a temporary job with the county prosecutor's office. I have known Harry Kim for more than forty years of his services to our county, and my relationship with him has always been amicable.

Andy first mentioned Harry Kim for the executive director's position at the executive committee meeting and then he mentioned the idea by e-mail to several board members. He also started quoting the infamous words of the CEO at committee meetings, "prohibit the executive director from making future program and financial commitments," in order to denounce me.

Also denouncing me by emphasizing the CEO's infamous quotation was Darwin Ching. He quoted that same comment in his response to Senator Akaka, who had requested the release of ARRA funds to HCEOC. He copied his response to the governor, lieutenant governor, senior policy advisor, and Sam Aiona, director of the Office of Community Services, as well as other elected and appointed officials—and the CEO's phrase spread.

Ching added another derogatory comment about our agency, too. He wrote that, according to an annual audit by an independent auditor, HCEOC had mismanaged $43,366 in federal funds. That was incorrect, though, and an error on the part of the agency's new auditor. The auditor's role was to conduct an agency audit for the period from October 1, 2007, to September 30, 2008, and did not include any programs beyond September 30th. Those funds in question were earmarked for contract work to be completed beyond September 30, the audit's fiscal year ending date. At the end date of performances, all contractors were paid as planned.

Andy Levin's proposal to hire Harry Kim was not enthusiastically accepted by board members, because, unlike the county government which has steady revenues, a non-profit community action agency has only a modicum of core funds and must first mobilize resources through advocacy and grant writing, and then implement projects with any funds mobilized. As I had long known, it's a tedious and difficult double job.

Andy had done Harry a disservice by recommending him to the unwanted position.

I did transition to the position of "resource mobilizer" in 2009, and I still do all the grant writing. I don't regret the change at all. I'll be eighty-nine years old this year, 2015, and it's about time to take it easy. When I was executive director, I was downstairs and upstairs twenty times a day, checking it all out and keeping track of everything, and it was a lot of work. Now I only go after the money.

Mobilizing the Resources

In late May 2009, in the midst of some chaos, I needed to organize an advocacy effort at the County Council budget hearing for $625,000 of transportation program funds, as we had done in the past. I mustered up about a dozen elderly women to attend the hearing and told them they could just occupy seats and need not say anything. Their presence was to gain the sympathy of the council members and render support to our request for funding.

The program funding did not come easily, though. Following the nation's economic recession, the Hawai'i County government was also experiencing a budget crunch, and council members were haggling over the county budget. But then courageous council member Donald Ikeda, a staunch supporter of our programs, recommended transferring funds from the legislative auditor's budget in order to grant us full funding of our transportation program. Despite protests from some council members, the council voted to fund our request in full. The elderly and the disabled were grateful to council member Ikeda for being instrumental in appropriation of the funds.

The next day, the *Hawaii Tribune-Herald* ran an article on the budget hearing. The reporter wrote that he asked one of the elderly woman why was she attending the hearing, and she replied, "I don't know." What should have been a short news story turned into an innuendo, suggesting that about a dozen elderly women were brought to the hearing without knowing why they were present. It was a cruel article.

> A little more than a year later, in July 2010, another *haole* reporter wrote about the same incident of the elderly woman saying, "I don't know" – again implying that the elderly women were brought in without knowing why there were there.

And again, the newspaper missed the finer aspects of our local culture. The elderly woman questioned by the reporter called me after she read the first article and apologized to me for her response. I consoled her and thanked her for being present at the budget hearing. I told her that the reporter's question was a stupid one, and therefore required a stupid answer, and told her that she responded to it correctly.

She explained that when a haole person asked her a difficult question, or one that required explaining, she usually answered, "I don't know," to free herself from having to try and answer in burdensome, standard English.

Also in May 2009, the House Committee on Finance held a legislative hearing for non-profit organizations to make grant-in-aid requests. It turned out, though, to merely be a ploy; the revised state statute required a public hearing for its legislative process.

The hearing was held at the state capitol auditorium and was attended by nearly one hundred and fifty applicants representing non-profit organizations. The chair of the Committee on Finance conducted the hearing and announced that there was a three-minute time limit per applicant. I asked whether the three-minute limit applied to each request, explaining that I had six grant applications, which would therefore total eighteen minutes. He responded that each non-profit organization had three minutes total.

I complained that I had flown to the meeting from Hilo and taken a taxi from the airport solely in order to testify. Being limited to thirty seconds per application defeated the purpose of the hearing. But the chair prevailed and the three-minute limit stood.

One of the hearing committee members told me that the chair learned that our agency received nearly one million dollars in ARRA funds, and that we were therefore in a better financial position than most of the other applicants—and that the committee subsequently recommended we receive zero funding. I realized, more than ever, how critical the ARRA funds were to our survival. I wondered whether our agency would be able to continue providing services for the Big Island's poor, and worried about my own earnest but selfish desire to contribute as I had been doing over a forty year period.

Particularly in 2009, that year of the "showdown," I took on the challenge with gusto and a renewed commitment to do what I could to bring an end to all the negative issues.

I called Sam Aiona and reminded him of the injustices his CSBG administrator caused me. I pointed out that her unfounded, seemingly derogatory and libelous remarks about our agency in her monitoring report caused a chain of reactions that resulted in serious problems. After lengthy consideration, I told him, I'd decided to consult with my attorney about filing a legal complaint.

Sam might have told the CSBG administrator of my intent; a few weeks later, whether by coincidence or otherwise, she found another job and left the state Office of Community Services.

Andy Levin, chair of our board, resigned in the third week of July 2009. He wrote, in an email to the executive committee: "I don't think George is the right person to be the executive director, and since he is determined to stay, it is better that I go."

It was an ethically questionable and equivocal statement. I never mentioned to him, nor to the executive committee, that I wanted to stay on as executive director, nor that Andy Levin asked me to step down and assume another position. What I said was that Darwin Ching would not approve the ARRA funds for HCEOC if I were still the executive director, and therefore I voluntarily agreed to step down.

The core of the matter was that Andy Levin did not want me to step down, but wanted me to resign from the agency altogether so he could maneuver someone of his choice into the executive director position. Unfortunately for him, he was unable to convince the board to oust me. To me, it played out like a grueling game of chess between Andy and me. I won.

However, I have no lasting animosity toward him. It was just politics used as a means to an end, for him and for me too, for that matter. I was the victor in that way, as well.

I am grateful to Marcella Stroh and Sandra "Sandy" Song, both members of the executive committee. They defended me and supported me throughout the ordeal.

Marcella, a senior vice president at Central Pacific Bank, became a critical cog in providing guidance to our fiscal department. She tirelessly attended our committee and board meetings and helped us to the extent that ARRA funds were approved for disbursement to our agency.

Sandy, an attorney and former District Court Judge, served in several capacities on our board—as a member, board chair, legal consultant, and friend—for more than twenty-five years. In September, Sandy was appointed interim executive director, I officially stepped down to assume the position of resource mobilizer, and Jay Kimura was elected board chair.

Sandy's primary efforts involved the release of ARRA funds to our agency and sustaining program activities with whatever funding was available. She was in constant contact with Darwin Ching and finally, in November 2009, he confirmed that our agency had made improvements to our fiscal department and that I had stepped down. Darwin recommended the governor release $903,563 in ARRA funds to HCEOC.

In anticipation of those ARRA funds, in January we hired twenty-one employees for our Language Arts Multicultural Program (LAMP) and our Dropout Prevention Program (DOPP). Most were former employees, then subsisting on unemployment benefits, and some were new employees.

However, HCEOC did not receive the funds.

In the second week of February, Sandy asked me to contact the governor's office and speak to whomever I knew well enough to ask for help getting the funds released; our programs had started in January and we direly needed the money. I immediately emailed Linda Smith, the governor's senior policy adviser, listing the facts that should have contributed to the funds' release:

- HCEOC's contract for ARRA CSBG allocations had been signed and approved by Darwin Ching, director of the Department of Labor and Industrial Relations, and Sam Aiona, executive director of the Office of Community Services, state administrators of the ARRA CSBG. The contract had been sent to Department of Budget and Finance for the director's recommendation prior to approval by the governor.
- The expiration date of the ARRA funds was September 30, 2010, which gave our agency a little more than seven months to implement the intended projects.
- Hawai'i's three community action agencies had received the funds in 2009. HCEOC was the only agency yet to receive the ARRA funds.
- The Recovery Act mandated that states pass through no less than ninety-nine percent of their grant allocations to eligible entities under the CSBG Act, commonly referred to as Community Action Agencies.

"Due to the factors mentioned above," I wrote, "your assistance in facilitating the release of funds would be greatly appreciated by both clients and staff of HCEOC."

Linda Smith responded by urging me to talk to Sam Aiona—but he was, unfortunately, unavailable. Therefore I contacted Kay Iwaliko, a manager I knew at the Department of Budget and Finance, and asked her about our ARRA contract.

Kay told me she would look into it and called me back within an hour. She told me the contract documents had been sent to the wrong office. They should have been submitted directly to the governor's office, she said, and told me she'd instructed Sam to pick up the documents at her office.

It was a big blunder on Sam Aiona's part, but an unintentional one. I surmised that the former CSBG administrator handled the contract documents for the other three community action agencies, and sent them to the proper office—the governor's office—but that he was not aware of this special procedure for ARRA grant documents, and incorrectly sent them to Budget and Finance (which was the usual route for grant documents).

When Sam retrieved our grant documents from Budget and Finance, he had to rewrite the cover letter, which was addressed to the Department of Budget and Finance, to the Office of the Governor, and he needed to get Darwin Ching's signature. A heated argument ensued. Darwin Ching, an impeccable follower of protocol, is said to have chastised Sam to such a degree that Sam resigned from his executive director's position on the spot.

The governor signed the contract and we received our first increment of funds within two weeks.

I find it ironic that those ARRA funds were the same ones we would not receive if I did not step down from the executive director position—but I was the very one instrumental in securing the release of those funds to our agency.

The Humiliation

In 2010, a year after I stepped down from the position of executive director at HCEOC, I was perturbed and extremely saddened when the board of directors voted to sell the Seiganji property at Captain Cook in Kona.

That one-acre property had been bequeathed to HCEOC in 1991 on the insistent and fervent recommendation of Reverend Hosho Totoki, the priestess of Kona Seiganji Shingon Mission, for our human services programs. It's located on a graduated slope overlooking the tranquil and picturesque Kealakekua Bay. The temple facilities consisted of an assembly hall, a meditation building, office, living quarters, and a large kitchen. It was an ideal example of a complex for human services programs, as well as a tangible asset for HCEOC.

We expanded our meal service program to the Kona district to serve the low-income elderly population by providing meals to the county-operated congregated meals program and also to childcare centers.

Other services we established were the U.S. Department of Agriculture surplus food distribution program to qualified low-income residents and the U.S. Department of Energy Low Income Home Energy Assistance Program, which helped qualified low-income residents pay electric bills; programs that benefitted nearly two thousand residents in Kona each year. HCEOC also used Seiganji for community district council board meetings.

The board of directors decided to sell Seiganji to defray the cost of some deficit spending, brought on by some very late disbursement of appropriated grant funds—both from the state Office of Community Services (OCS) of the federal CSBG funds, which were to be passed through by state OCS to our agency, and the state grant-in-aid funds, also disbursed by the state OCS, which were overdue by six months.

As executive director I'd faced the exact same critical situation three times, and each time, I'd handled it by temporarily terminating the employment of all employees of the affected programs. I asked them to apply for unemployment benefits and promised to recall them to work once funds became available. They willingly agreed. Many told me that being laid off was like a vacation, with the comforting knowledge that their bi-weekly income continued, via the unemployment checks, and that they would be called back to work. This worked—our agency survived, and we never took drastic action such as selling off tangible assets.

However, it was for naught. I pleaded with the board to temporarily lay off employees until the program funds were disbursed, but they did not and the sale of Seiganji went through. I was very saddened by it.

Several weeks later, my sister, Kay, asked me, in an anxious voice, "Why did you sell Seiganji?" I told her I did not have the power to override the board's decision but I had strongly recommended they retain the property.

Kay told me it was only proper and decent to inform Reverend Hosho Totoki of the sale. Kay felt great remorse, as she was the one who had first told Reverend Totoki about HCEOC and its Human Services program back when Reverend Totoki said she was retiring. Reverend Totoki had been looking for an organization to carry on meaningful human services to Kona's elderly and poor; she wanted to recommend such an organization to the mission's trustees and suggest they transfer the Seiganji to such an organization by a warranty deed. She chose HCEOC.

Soon after, my sister brought Reverend Totoki to see me in Hilo. Reverend Totoki mentioned that it had been nineteen years since HCEOC acquired Seiganji, and she was appalled to learn that HCEOC had sold the property. She was polite, but emphatically asked me why.

I could only respond with a feeble reply that was totally inadequate. I told her I was no longer in charge. The current board of directors, the ones making the policy, had decided to sell Seiganji to defray the cost of the agency's programs.

With every question she asked, I apologized. There were no good answers to her inquiries. In my entire life, I had never felt so humiliated.

Reverend Hosho Totoki (center)

Only a very few weeks later, the grant funds started trickling in. They culminated in our receiving President Obama's American Recovery and Reinvestment Act (ARRA) funds totaling nearly a million dollars. The sale of Seiganji turned out to be completely unnecessary. I feel so much regret about it.

Chapter 29. My Last Political Hurrah

With the 2010 governor's election upon us, Congressman Neil Abercrombie came to my office in March with a small group of supporters, Gilbert "Gil" Kahele and Lloyd Nekoba among them. I was very familiar with Gil, who had campaigned for Dan Akaka in his successful bid for Congress and for Ben Cayetano for governor. Lloyd was also a friend; he had campaigned for Jean Kim for lieutenant governor and Ben Cayetano for both lieutenant governor and governor.

Congressman Abercrombie asked me to support him and I replied, "How could I not support you?" I reminded him of our LAMP and dropout prevention program funding, which he singlehandedly made happen by convincing conference committee members to appropriate the funds during his term as a state senator.

From that day, I was a member of the Abercrombie for Governor campaign team but I had some doubts as to whether I could be effective. I was no longer in charge of the county-wide grassroots campaign network I had organized nearly forty years before, which went hand-in-hand with our advocacy for the community action programs. I was truly unsure whether or not the grassroots of nearly fifteen hundred people would rally around me this time, as they had in the past, but I was committed to try.

On the Republican side, in the meantime, Lieutenant Governor James Aiona announced his candidacy for governor, as expected. A few weeks after that, Mayor Mufi Hannemann came by seeking my support. He announced his candidacy for governor while simultaneously resigning from his Honolulu mayor's seat. Going as far as resigning from his mayor position in order to run for governor told me he felt very confident about winning.

I had to decline from supporting him, though, since I had already committed my support to Neil Abercrombie. With Mufi in the race, we were facing a grueling campaign for the primary election.

The unions gave Mufi an intimidating amount of support. He received endorsements from seventeen public and private unions—foremost, the Hawaiʻi Government Employees Association (HGEA), which was the largest public union in the state; the equally powerful United Public Workers Union; and the International Longshoremen Workers Union (ILWU), which is still the largest private industry union.

The only large, notable union to endorse Neil Abercrombie was the Hawaiʻi State Teacher Association (HSTA), although a few smaller ones endorsed him, too.

And so the Abercrombie for Governor campaign was organized.

Gil Kahele was campaign chair for the Big Island, along with Yoshito Takamine, Eusebio (Bobo) Lapenia, Margaret Ushijima, Janet Fujioka, and Sandy Song as honorary chairs. Dwight Takamine was unanimously appointed to be campaign coordinator, leading a steering committee composed of fifteen members experienced in campaign work, who were assigned duties such as putting up yard signs, house-to-house canvassing, person-to-person contacts, fundraising, sign-waving, community meetings, publicity, and campaign headquarters administration and grassroots.

Meanwhile, Sandy Song stepped down as interim executive director of HCEOC after her demanding and exhausting—but ultimately successful—efforts for the release of ARRA funds. She went on to resume her private law practice.

Lester Seto, our community services director, was appointed interim executive director of HCEOC in April 2010. I had known Lester since 1972, when he was hired as a youth program coordinator at HCEOC. It was under his leadership that we operated our race relations program and dropout prevention program for at-risk high school students. Later he was promoted to Head Start program director. Lester had helped me in many political campaigns, starting with George Ariyoshi for governor and Dan Akaka for Congress.

After several years of serving HCEOC, he returned to the U.S. mainland to resume his role as an ordained Christian minister. Midway into the first decade of the new century, he returned to Hilo to look after his ailing mother. At that time, I hired him as our community services director, and then he was appointed as interim executive director of HCEOC.

I was overjoyed when Lester Seto, Sandy Song, the new board chair Jay Kimura, and board members Marcella Stroh and Gerald DeMello, who was community relations director of the University of Hawai'i at Hilo, joined the Abercrombie campaign. I knew this would rejuvenate our grassroots effort and contribute to a victorious campaign for Neil.

Dwight Takamine's strategy was to solidify the grassroots in order to counterbalance the strong, opposing labor union force that was based on campaigning for union-endorsed candidates each election year. To this end, he proposed an HCEOC fundraiser consisting of people sponsoring a testimonial for me, based on my nearly forty years of service to this island's disadvantaged people.

In My Honor

Sandy and Dwight, both attorneys, researched the Federal Hatch Act first, so we did not run afoul of laws regarding political activities conducted by non-profit organizations, and found our fundraiser to be in compliance.

Under Dwight's leadership, they formed a planning committee made-up of HCEOC staff, board members, union representatives, and friends of HCEOC. The committee met for six months to plan and organize the testimonial.

Dwight served as master of ceremonies at the 2010 event, which started with people "roasting" me: President of the State Senate Colleen Hanabusa, County Mayor Billy Kenoi, and Congressman Neil Abercrombie. I was surprised that about fifteen hundred grassroots people showed up.

Mayor Kenoi said that I drove around in a twenty-year-old, rusty, compact car, and thus, as an executive director of poverty programs, set a good example. The roast pleased the crowd and brought a lot of laughter.

There were video messages from our U.S. Senators, about two minutes each, that showed on a wide screen. Senator Akaka's speech was warm and comforting; he said things such as, "George is like a brother to me" and recollected our personal relationship since 1971. He emphasized our identical commitments to help the needy.

Senator Dan Inouye's speech sounded like he was making up for years of uncertainty about me and HCEOC. It was full of comments like, "George Yokoyama did this" and "George Yokoyama did that," and he showered me with accolades. I was truly honored by his remarks.

I first met Senator Inouye back in 1975, when Kazuo (Kazu) Komura, Governor Ariyoshi's liaison officer, introduced us at the side entrance of Hilo's Afook-Chinen Civic Auditorium. I put out my arm to shake his hand and was surprised to see that he kept his arm at his side. He looked me up and down—from my unpolished shoes to my faded aloha shirt and my head that needed a haircut—inspecting me the same way one might look at a local bum. I was about to withdraw my arm when he slowly extended his and we shook hands. Neither of us spoke, and then he entered the auditorium with Kazu.

Kazu came looking for me about fifteen minutes later and told me the senator had a dim memory of meeting me before, and had been trying to recall when and where it was. Kazu told him I had only recently returned to Hilo after more than twenty years abroad; he could not have met me. He also told the senator that I helped with the 1974 Ariyoshi campaign for governor by mobilizing the Hawaiian and Filipino votes that contributed to his overall victory, despite his losing on Oʻahu to Frank Fasi.

Another memorable encounter with Dan Inouye had changed everything for the best. Around 2003, he'd been a guest at a Hawaiʻi Community Action Directors Association meeting being held in the conference room of the Honolulu Community Action program. Four executive directors and four board chairs of the state's community action agencies were present, and they were discussing the state's human service programs with the senator.

During the intermission, I went to the hallway where there was coffee, orange juice, and pastries. As I poured myself some coffee, Senator Inouye stopped by for a glass of orange juice.

"How's the Big Island doing?" he asked.

"Not so good," I told him. "The economy is in bad shape with the sugar industry in bankruptcy, and there are no new industries foreseen to take the place of sugar." But I thanked him for the tremendous help he had been in alleviating economic hardships for the unemployed and the poor of our county.

He amazed me by asking me about our Language Arts Multicultural Program and dropout prevention program, as well as the welfare-to-work program recently awarded by the U.S. Department of Labor. He told me that HCEOC was the only grantee in the state to receive the award. It astonished me that he knew so much about our agency, our transportation program for the elderly and disabled, and our job training and placement programs. I surmised that one of our other congressional delegates, Senator Matsunaga, Senator Akaka, or Congresswoman Mink, who had communication with our agency, must have told him about our programs.

Senator Inouye had great knowledge of the needs, problems, and interventions being carried out in our communities.

Dr. Abercrombie

At the testimonial held in my honor, Dwight Takamine called upon me to address the well-wishers. I thanked everyone who had helped so much, and subtly expounded on the political for followers of Neil Abercrombie:

I especially express my gratitude to Dr. Neil Abercrombie, not because he is a candidate for governor, but because of what he has done for the people of the Big Island.

From 1975 to 1982, for seven years, we operated two educational programs, a language arts multicultural program for elementary school students, and a high school drop-out prevention program with federal grant funds. But in 1982, we were informed that non-profit organizations were no longer eligible to compete for grants.

Therefore, we looked to the state legislature to fund the programs. Bills were introduced, committee hearings were held and referred to the House and Senate money committees for final appropriation of funds. Our bills were killed in the House, but kept alive by the Senate. Members of the conference committee confided in me, saying that our bills were dead on arrival.

> But then, something of a miracle happened. Dr. Abercrombie sent memos to each committee member, and eloquently and convincingly advocated for our programs. Funding was appropriated, and Governor Ariyoshi released the funds.
>
> After thirty-five years, the programs still continue with more than twelve thousand students and an additional eighteen thousand two hundred parents and guardians, for a total of more than thirty thousand people of this Big Island touched by the programs.
>
> Dr. Abercrombie, a fleeting moment of decision-making turned out to be years and years of services and benefits to the people.
>
> Dr. Abercrombie, the people of the Big Island are grateful to you, HCEOC employees are grateful to you, and I am grateful to you. I ask all of you for a resounding applause for Dr. Abercrombie.
>
> ...The war on poverty has not ended. It still goes on. More so, in this period of economic stagnation. This county has the distinction of having the highest percentage of individuals on public assistance, highest percentage of Supplemental Nutrition Assistance Program recipients, and the highest unemployment rate in the entire state....

I purposely addressed Neil as "Dr. Abercrombie" to promote his status as an educated person to the elderly Asians, especially the Japanese, who value and respect individuals with a doctor's degree as the epitome of success and the highest possible rank in society.

Two elderly Japanese women came up to me at the end of the program, and one said, "I didn't know that he had a doctor's degree. I thought he was a hippie."

The other woman said, "We will campaign for Dr. Abercrombie."

Those comments reassured me that I'd done the right thing, and after that night I always referred to Neil as "Dr. Abercrombie" at community meetings where older Asians people were present.

The testimonial was a success. I was elated to observe that most people stayed until the end of the program. Some of the notable individuals that came from other islands to attend included former Governor George Ariyoshi, who was called upon to give a short speech; his son Donn from Oʻahu; Representative Joseph Souki from Maui, speaker emeritus of the state House of Representatives; Mabel Fujiuchi, executive director of Kauaʻi Economic Opportunity; Gladys Baisa, former executive director of Maui Economic Opportunity; Sandy Baz, current executive director of Maui Economic Opportunity; Brian Schatz, candidate for lieutenant governor; and my good friend Chuck Freedman, from Oʻahu.

But most noticeable was how many of our program clients attended, including some of the elderly from our transportation program, parents from our elementary and high school educational programs, individuals from our job training program, and former and current employees of our agency.

After the testimonial I felt honored and grateful when a ninety-two-year-old woman named Haruko Yoshina put a *kukui* nut lei around my neck. It was a fitting end to the event and the start of our grassroots campaign for Neil Abercrombie.

Business Participation

At the onset of our campaigning, I felt there was one segment of the campaign organization that needed to be enhanced, and that was the participation of the business sector.

Roland Higashi was a businessman I'd campaigned with before. He had managed and participated in many victorious campaigns, including two for Ariyoshi for governor, two for Steven Yamashiro for mayor, and he also participated on the steering committees of the John Waihee and the Ben Cayetano gubernatorial campaigns, as well as Billy Kenoi for mayor. His candidate won every single time.

Once when Neil Abercrombie visited Hilo, I met Neil, Roland, and Roland's wife, Jan, at a downtown restaurant and we talked for about two hours. Roland and Jan committed to supporting Neil Abercrombie at that meeting. I was finally satisfied we had a hard-hitting campaign team, complete with business, grassroots, and inroads to a labor union.

Right after that, Roland and Jan organized a successful fundraiser gathering at the Naniloa Hotel for upper- and middle-class business people. Along with Bobo Lapenia and other campaign team members, they also organized a Filipino gathering at Nani Mau Gardens, which was also successful. It was a big help to the Abercrombie campaign that Roland and Jan contacted their friends from the middle- and upper-classes, because most of them were unreachable by our grassroots. They also provided two buses in order to increase attendance by Hilo supporters at a Kona campaign rally for Abercrombie.

Although our opponent Mufi Hannemann was endorsed by the ILWU, I was optimistic that the retired ILWU sugar plantation workers would support Neil Abercrombie—because most of the ILWU pensioners still resided in former plantation camps and were clients of our transportation program. We had more than seven thousand elderly clients in our transportation program, and the vast majority were former ILWU members. At each community meeting where ILWU pensioners were present, I mentioned former ILWU leaders Yoshito Takamine and Bobo Lapenia, both supporters of Neil. I extolled their accomplishments during the heydays of union power when they raised take-home pay and improved working conditions for the workers. The pensioners remembered and still considered Yoshito and Bobo to be their leaders. Most of the retired workers sided with Yoshito and Bobo, and therefore supported Neil Abercrombie.

Visiting Miloliʻi

Several months after the Hilo testimonial event, Gil Kahele, the Big Island chair of the Abercrombie for Governor campaign, came up with a plan to hold another testimonial at the Hawaiian fishing village at Miloliʻi, which was on the outskirts of Kona and where Gil was born and raised. There were two goals for the testimonial: to commend me for mobilizing funds for the construction of those forty-four new homes with photovoltaic power, which provided decent and comfortable living for a population of about two hundred and fifty people; and, more importantly, as a campaign gathering for Neil Abercrombie.

Bobo Lapenia drove us to Miloliʻi in his SUV. Also with us were Jimmy Imai, our official Hilo campaign headquarters cook, and Glen Hisashima, a retired captain of Kūlani State Prison.

We arrived at Miloliʻi about three hours before the testimonial. Neil Abercrombie, who had flown into Kailua-Kona and was driven to Miloliʻi, arrived at about the same time. Gil owned a second home in Miloliʻi and invited us over, since we had ample time before the testimonial.

Neil said, "I need the exercise; let's walk." It was about a three-quarter mile walk to Gil's house along a narrow, asphalted black road that ran through a lava field.

As we walked, Neil told me how wonderful it was to live in Hawai'i among such a diversity of ethnic groups, and as if to accentuate the meaning of what he said, he uttered the words, "Diversity makes one." He was referring to the distinct culture that had evolved here, with all ethnic groups contributing a part of their culture to the pan-Hawai'i culture we affectionately

refer to as "local culture," where ethnic groups live harmoniously together. I do not remember if he used those exact words, but his thoughts were almost identical to what I preached for years in our Language Arts Multicultural Program.

I knew I grasped the essence of his meaning and I was thrilled with his remark, which suddenly made me realize he was one of us. His phrase, "Diversity makes one," became etched indelibly in my mind.

The Hawaiians at Miloli'i were friendly. Neil had a wonderful time making friends and I doubted that an opposition candidate would ever come down to that village. He had a captive crowd in Miloli'i, all to himself.

Meeting with the Grassroots

Several months before the election, we started our community grassroots campaign meetings, with former and current clients of all our agency's programs attending. The exclusive purpose of the meetings was to commit votes for Neil Abercrombie. We concentrated on East Hawai'i and provided grassroots support to John Buckstead and his wife, Pat, who had planted their roots in Kona. They were experienced in community organization work and assumed leadership for the campaign in West Hawai'i. I felt Kona was in good hands.

I always concluded these meetings by asking, "Will you help us?" The crowd always answered, "Yes." Then I told them how they could truly help: by contacting their friends and relatives and asking them to vote for Neil Abercrombie.

We held our first meeting in Hilo. I picked on three clients and asked, "How many friends and relatives do you have?" After thinking a few minutes, one reported twenty friends and forty relatives, another said ten friends and thirty relatives, still another said fifty friends and sixty relatives, for a total of two hundred and ten. I told the audience of fifty that the average person could contact seventy people. If the fifty people at that meeting each contacted seventy people, I said, then that meant reaching three thousand five hundred friends and relatives. I reminded them to contact their parents and grandparents, brothers and sisters, uncles and aunties, cousins, nieces and nephews, their in-laws, and their friends to vote for Neil Abercrombie.

I asked them to submit the names, addresses, and telephone numbers of their friends and relatives who committed to vote for Neil Abercrombie, as well as those who volunteered to work for the campaign. I told them that campaign workers would call the people on the list to thank them and to offer complimentary tickets to Abercrombie's fundraiser at the Civic Auditorium.

From past campaign experience, I knew that people's daily routine was to come home from work, watch the TV news, have dinner, take a bath, turn on the television set again for favorite programs, and then go to bed. I knew that working people simply could not make much time for calling on the phone. I advised them to set aside fifteen to thirty minutes each day, which would make contacting a few people per day manageable.

I told the group that all contacts needed to be made, and lists of confirmed supporters turned in, within thirty days. Finally I said, "Can we count on you?" The meeting concluded with a resounding "Yes!"

Names of people committed to voting for Neil Abercrombie came pouring in. For some of the retired elderly, trying to get people to commit became a pleasant pastime. Within ten days, they had contacted all of their friends and relatives and submitted their names, telephone numbers, and addresses to us, including those who committed to help by becoming campaign workers. We gathered more than four thousand names of Abercrombie-committed voters.

We conducted four additional community meetings, one each in Hāmākua, Keaʻau, Pāhala and Nāʻālehu, all with the same results, though with fewer committed voters because we had fewer program clients in outlying areas. We amassed three thousand five hundred committed votes from the four community meetings, for a grand total of more than seven thousand five hundred when we included Hilo.

Because the big labor unions were endorsing our opponent, we could not use their large union halls and facilities and had to rent public school cafeterias and community centers for our meetings, but we accomplished our mission. One of our main objectives was to get the candidates running for other offices to rally around Abercrombie.

The Big Day, 2010

Finally, Primary Election Day arrived. Neil Abercrombie won in every precinct except one in Hilo, which he lost by very little. In the general election, Abercrombie won in every single Hawai'i County precinct. Both the primary and general elections were wipeout victories, and it was very satisfying that the grassroots helped him become governor of the state of Hawai'i in order to benefit the poor.

I expected that election to be my last political hurrah. But like a punch-drunk pugilist, when the gong sounds, I may rise up to fight another round or two of a grassroots political battle.

Chapter 30. The Media, Unions, and Others

With the exception of only a few fabricated innuendoes throughout the years, the news media generally ran articles about our agency and programs that portrayed a positive public image and good community support.

Hugh Clark, of *The Honolulu Advertiser*, wrote many community interest stories about our agency throughout the years. They were always factual and newsworthy and resulted in community awareness and support. After he retired, Gordon Pang took over, and he, too, always quoted me accurately.

Political columnist Richard Borreca, of the former *Honolulu Star-Bulletin*, wrote about my personal involvement in political elections with straightforward reporting and accurate, verbatim quotes. Rod Thompson, also of the *Star-Bulletin*, covered our agency's newsworthy stories, quoting me accurately, and Hunter Bishop of the *Hawaii Tribune-Herald* covered us accurately and positively as well.

All these reporters practiced ethical journalism, and their fact-oriented articles were straightforward and free of implied, subtle innuendoes.

We sometimes had a difficult relationship with the public government workers' unions, particularly with rank-and-file members and especially when pocketbook issues of cuts in pay and fringe benefits came to the fore, generally prior to the governor's second term of office. The public unions' leadership may officially endorse the incumbent, despite budget woes, but in protest the rank-and-file members tended to support the opposition candidate. This was the case with Governor Cayetano, who won his second term of office, fortunately, but only by a very small margin of votes; he lost on the Big Island by a whopping five thousand votes.

Generally, though, we had an amicable relationship with the public unions, and many times we supported the candidates they endorsed because that candidate supported programs benefitting our island's low-income population. We were fortunate that all our elected officials supported funding our county-wide programs, as well as projects for a single specific district.

Republican Representative Virginia Isbell of the Kona district successfully introduced the bill to fund our self-help housing development project at Miloliʻi, where all residents were low-income. She switched parties and became a Democrat, and again was able to appropriate funds for water development at Miloliʻi.

Representative Harvey Tajiri of Hilo was instrumental in appropriating funds to construct our agency's central complex facilities on a five-acre parcel of state land on Rainbow Drive.

Representative Jerry Chang, who at that time represented Puna, appropriated funds for construction of a Head Start center at Hawaiian Beaches.

When Jerry Chang moved to the Hilo district, Representative Helene Hale represented Puna, and she successfully appropriated funds for our Kīkala-Keōkea housing project for Kalapana lava flow victims on one hundred fifty acres of state land.

After Helene passed away, Representative Faye Hanohano became the new State Representative for the Puna district. She served on the Committee on Finance and helped us tremendously by voting for appropriation of all of our grant requests.

Representative Robert Herkes was successful in appropriating funds for the replacement of water tanks for Miloliʻi, and supported all our other appropriation requests as well.

Finally, Representative Dwight Takamine ensured that all our funding requests passed, throughout his tenure as chair of the Committee on Finance, including periodic funding of ten buses at a time for our transportation program.

As for senators, I had personal contact with John Ushijima, Stanley Hara, Richard Henderson, Dante Carpenter, Malama Solomon, Wayne Metcalf, Richard Matsuura, Russell Kokubun, and Josh Green, who always supported us in the Senate, and passed funding requests approved by the House.

From the other islands, our funding requests were supported by Speakers of the House Henry Peters, Richard Kawakami, Danny Kihano, Joe Souki, and Calvin Say. I was privileged to have had personal contacts with them.

I also made many friendly acquaintances with lawmakers from other islands, which resulted in support for our program funding. Among the most influential lawmakers was Senator Norman Mizuguchi, former Senate president who played basketball for the Hilo High School Vikings. Whenever the Vikings were in town for the state tournament, Senator Mizuguchi went to root for his alma mater. He had a PhD in education and a keen interest in our Language Arts Multicultural Program. He visited Hilo, met with our LAMP staff, and treated them to lunch at Restaurant Fuji. From them, he learned the finer points of helping underachieving students become independent thinkers.

Senator Ann Kobayashi was former chair of the Senate Committee on Ways and Means, the money committee. Mike Amii, the trusted right hand of political campaign guru Bob Oshiro, introduced us, and Ann committed to support our funding requests not because of my urgings, but because Mike was her staunch supporter. I was grateful that things turned out for the best.

It was when the world was preoccupied with the news of New York City's Twin Towers disaster, in September 2001, that a friend quietly arrived on the shores of Kailua-Kona. It was John Buckstead, whom I mentioned earlier. He was a former staff member of the Office of Economic Opportunity (OEO), presently known as the Office of Community Services (OCS), under the U.S. Department of Health and Human Services.

He and several other courageous individuals accomplished what I considered a heroic feat: they filed a lawsuit against President Richard Nixon for attempting to dismantle the OEO, which had been established by President Johnson. Ultimately, the court agreed that Nixon's dismantling of OEO was unconstitutional, and thus the OEO, forerunner to the OCS, was saved.

After he retired from government services, John served as executive director of the National Association of Community Action Agencies in Washington, D.C., and then he finally retired and came to our island with his wife, Pat. They purchased a home in Kailua and became permanent residents, intending to spend the rest of their life basking in Kailua's sun and balmy weather.

But what actually happened was that his arrival meant there was an infusion of new blood into our war on poverty. Soon after they arrived, John and Pat came by our Hilo office on Rainbow Drive, and we took a walk around his old haunts. John vividly remembered the area from Rainbow Falls up to the old Hilo Memorial Hospital, which long ago had been converted to a Peace Corps training center where he had trained before his assignment overseas.

Feeling nostalgic, he looked for a plaque he remembered near the entrance to the former Peace Corps center, and was disappointed to find it was gone. In a solemn voice, he uttered the John F. Kennedy quote he said had been inscribed on the plaque: "Ask not what your country can do for you; ask what you can do for your country."

I revised the words to fit our local situation and murmured to myself, "Ask what I can do for the disadvantaged people of our island." I, too, was in a thoughtful mood and it strengthened my resolve to help people.

John and Pat quickly assimilated into our local community. They registered to vote and became members of the Hawai'i County Democratic party, and became politically involved in advocating for the poor. Within a short time, John was elected chair of our county's Democratic party.

Chapter 31. The Hawaiians

When I reflect on my long-ago meeting with the elderly sensei in northern Japan, and the commitment I made to be kind, respectful, and helpful to the Hawaiian people, I am gratified to realize that our agency served many tens of thousands of Hawaiians during the nearly forty years of my tenure in its leadership role.

However, I was only able to fulfill part of my promise. Although I did provide services to the educationally, socially, and economically disadvantaged Hawaiians through our antipoverty programs for children and youth to adults and the elderly, I did not achieve the rest of my goal to the degree I would have liked. Regrettably, I was only of sparse assistance to Hawaiians in terms of their being appointed or elected to political leadership positions in local, state and federal governments.

The few Hawaiians I assisted in elections were: Daniel Akaka, U.S. House of Representatives and later U.S. Senator; John Waihee, Lieutenant Governor and later Governor, State of Hawai'i; Malama Solomon, Trustee, Office of Hawaiian Affairs and later State Senator; Kalani Schutte, Member and Chair, Hawai'i County Council; Robert Makuakane, Member, Hawai'i County Council; Billy Kenoi, Mayor, County of Hawai'i, and Faye Hanohano, State House of Representatives.

Fay Hanohano is controversial, but she's honest. She speaks from the heart and says what she's thinking. I used to wave signs for her on the highway and in the rain.

We also assisted the following Hawaiians, who were appointed by the governor to the State Commission on Hawaiian Home Lands: Aunty Abbie Napeahi, who was one of our agency's board directors; Ann

Nathaniel, also a board member of our agency; and Eleanor Ahuna, my Hilo High School classmate.

Aside from political leadership, though, a bonding friendship developed between myself and many Hawaiians who were outspoken about Hawaiian issues and offered rational solutions to issues, and active participation in projects that alleviated problems and helped with needs for Hawaiians.

One of those remarkable individuals was Charles "Charlie" Rose, a retired police captain who worked for me for several years as a division director. Outwardly, Charlie was a jolly fellow—his nickname was "Good Time Charlie"—yet when the discussion was about Hawaiians and Hawaiian issues, he abruptly changed his demeanor. He relished his participation.

He was active and energetic. He took the initiative to inform and educate Hawaiians about the newly established state Office of Hawaiian Affairs (OHA) by conducting community meetings. Trustees were elected by eligible Hawaiians to the OHA board, simultaneously with regular political elections, but Hawaiians were required to register separately for the OHA trustee ballot. Charlie begged me to help him organize community meetings around this, and I did.

He founded the Laupāhoehoe Hawaiian Civic Club and eventually moved to Honolulu to accept a position with the federal public defender's office. Even after he moved he continued working on projects for Hawaiians, such as establishing a credit union for Hawaiians and creating a *maile* cultivation project. He got the State Association of Hawaiian Civic Clubs involved in many efforts that benefitted Hawaiians.

When I visited Honolulu for work-related meetings—such as monthly meetings of the Hawaii Public Housing Authority, of which I was a board member, or my frequent visits to legislators with funding requests—I called Charlie or Mike Amii, whoever was available, to pick me up at the airport, and we usually had breakfast. With Mike, the breakfast conversation was generally on our state's political pulse. With Charlie, it was always about Hawaiian issues.

Sovereignty Bill

That Senator Akaka's Hawaiian sovereignty bill passed in the House several times, but stalled in the Senate, was a big issue with Charlie. Charlie knew that Senator Akaka was a personal friend of mine, and he pleaded with me to talk to the senator's office about the numerous amendments that were hampering the bill's passage in the Senate. Charlie recommending adopting the original bill without additional amendments, as passed by the House. Once it became an act, then the bill could be amended, following the example of the Native Alaskan Bill, which was amended more than thirty times after it passed.

I called James Sakai, Senator Akaka's chief of staff, and relayed that message, but, unfortunately, the Akaka Bill did not pass.

I wondered why Senator Inouye, with all his power, could not help. I have my own ideas about that. He was the big boss—President pro tempore, third in line for succession to the presidency after the vice president and Speaker of the House. Maybe he didn't want Akaka to get the credit.

Mililani Trask assisted me in beneficial projects for Hawaiians. She established the non-profit Gibson Foundation in Hilo for the promotion of housing for Hawaiians and assisted me with our self-help housing projects at Miloli'i, and on Hawaiian Home Lands in Keaukaha and Pana'ewa. She attended our self-help housing meetings and, using her background as an attorney, advised leaseholders on the legal aspects and the dos and don'ts of owning a home.

She also helped us by drafting the bill for one hundred and fifty acres of state-owned Kikala-Keokea homestead land, where Kalapana lava flow victims could rebuild their homes. Mililani, a few victims, and I testified at the state legislature. The bill was approved and forwarded to Governor Waihee. On the day of the deadline for signing bills, Governor Waihee called me at home at 10:30 p.m. and told me that he would sign. I thanked him on behalf of the Hawaiians who lost their homes to the lava.

But, he added, we would have to veto the bingo bill. This was a bill that came about when Speaker of the House Joe Souki wanted to alleviate the doldrums of inactivity at senior centers. He believed that many seniors were gamblers at heart, that bingo would create some excitement for them, and that attendance at senior centers would increase.

Unlike the well-heeled retirees of government services, though, many were pensioners from the plantations, had small retirement income, and could not afford a trip to Las Vegas.

Joe asked me to testify for the bingo bill at the House committee hearings and I did, but the bill was denied. He introduced the bill for four consecutive years, and finally, during the fourth year, Representative Wayne Metcalf, chair of the Committee on Judiciary, approved it and passed the bill out of his committee. In 1991, it was finally enacted by both the House and Senate and forwarded to Governor Waihee—who vetoed it.

It was a small sacrifice in exchange for the one hundred fifty acres of state land for Kalapana lava flow victims. Several times after that, the governor called me "The Bingo Kid."

Mililani also led the eight thousand members of Ka Lāhui, a Hawaiian sovereignty movement that expounded a "nation within a nation" concept of sovereignty, which I considered a rational solution to the issue.

Senator Clayton Hee was another remarkable Hawaiian I worked with. Although I only met him occasionally and had short conversations with him, I felt a spirit of congeniality between us that made me feel good—especially when he told me he would fully support me in anything I needed from the legislature. I was truly grateful for his kind words.

Charlie Rose told me that Clayton gave an eloquent and moving speech at the blessing of the establishment of the Native Hawaiians Roll Call Commission (Kanaʻiolowalu), and added that Clayton Hee would make an excellent governor in future years. Whether or not they were friends, I do not know. Charlie never mentioned Clayton during our conversations over the years, but he must have been truly impressed with Clayton's speech.

Throughout the years, I did indeed befriend many Hawaiians. In fact, I realize I have more Hawaiian friends than friends from any other ethnic group.

The Input

In the late 1970s, I visited Congressman Dan Akaka at his office in Washington, D.C. It happened that Myron Thompson, a Bishop Estate trustee at the time, happened to be visiting Dan then, too. Dan introduced us and invited me to join them for dinner.

While we ate, we talked about lifting Hawaiians up from the lowest rungs of the economic and social ladders, and then the conversation turned to the need to educate Hawaiians on sovereignty issues. I said that Hawai'i's population had evolved into a multicultural one, comprised of multiethnic people living in harmony amongst each other. The advocacy for sovereignty should be led by Hawaiians, I said, but it should include the support of all ethnic groups living in Hawai'i, so that all people would be in unison and reaching consensus in support of solutions.

Myron looked at Dan, while simultaneously pointing a finger at me, and replied, "He's right." I felt good to have made some input into the Hawaiian sovereignty issue that had not yet officially surfaced as the Akaka Bill.

The Hawaiians are my babies. A long time ago, after the old man told me to and after I came back to Hawai'i, I made a commitment: I've got to help the Hawaiians.

Chapter 32. Politics and The Future

I conclude this look back at my life by reemphasizing the adage, "Politics is a means to an end."

On the county and state levels, working on political elections to elect candidates who support our agency's goals has been the only sure way to mobilize program funds. On the national level, electing candidates who support the retention of the Community Services Block Grant funds, our agency's core monetary support, assured us that competitive grants for eligible non-profit organizations would continue to be available.

However, there is a deeper problem and reason behind there being so much need in Hawai'i County. For more than twenty years now, since the demise of the sugar industry, we have established no new industries of the same magnitude, and it is directly related to this that the island continues to endure a multitude of social problems.

Since the sugar plantations closed down in the late 1990s, Hawai'i County continues to have the highest unemployment rate and the highest number of food stamp and welfare recipients in the state. To rub salt into the wound, so to speak, this county, with the state's lowest per capita income, has one of the highest residential electricity rates in both the state and country. Many commodities on the island are more expensive including gasoline, imported food items, building materials, and other items because of additional high shipment costs from O'ahu and the mainland.

But the most critical problem caused by the Big Island's lack of new industry is the out-migration of potentially capable young adults after graduation from high school to pursue higher education elsewhere. Upon completing their mainland educations, many find a good-paying job away, get married, produce offspring, and do not return to the Big Island, unless it is much later when they hit retirement age.

What can we do to make more good jobs available here?

Starting around 1997, the demographics of the island's public school population, from Grades K to 12, has undergone a dramatic change, as well. Hawaiians have become the most numerous population, at forty percent. They are followed by Filipino students at fifteen percent, white students at fourteen percent, and Japanese at eight percent. Another ten percent is comprised of Koreans, Chinese, Southeast Asians, and other Pacific Islanders. The rest of the student population is comprised of Micronesians at six percent, Hispanics at four percent and Portuguese at three percent.

People think the Hawaiians are the minorities. Right now, when they're young, yes. But when they graduate, no. That's the day I'm waiting for!

With this demographic change, I envision a glimmer of hope for the Hawaiians. They are again becoming the majority population of these islands, which means that more Hawaiians will be elected to positions of political leadership. Perhaps some of the contention over the overthrow of the Hawaiian kingdom will be addressed, hopefully leading toward more congenial relationships within this multiethnic society of Hawai'i.

It has been more than five years since HCEOC had a permanent executive director. It's hard to find the right person to be permanent director.

The person must have emotional intelligence. When you deal with people, the most important thing is that you possess emotional intelligence. The workers have to feel like they're part of the game, and then once you assign them to the work, don't do it grudgingly but because they want to. They take ownership of the project and they feel proud. *I did it!* That kind of workmanship is up to them. You bring people in and train them the right way. You have to let them take ownership; then they do a good job.

After several turnovers, we have Jay Kimura serving as HCEOC's interim director. I have come to realize that Jay possesses the abilities needed in an executive director to an unusual degree. He gained these qualities from his more than thirty years of experience in personnel and programmatic administration as Hawai'i County prosecutor. My hope that he continues as HCEOC's permanent executive director has only become stronger as time went on.

Tom Brown is Jay's deputy director. He was director of the county's mass transit program and long demonstrated his executive competency in that arena.

That old man in Japan that I called Sensei, he really hit me, you know. He was right. It was wrong what I learned in elementary school. The teachers told us that Hawai'i requested the U.S. to annex it. Come on! Why did they lie to us in the public schools? I had to find out from an old Japanee man?! He was really right.

Something happened. In life, sometimes something happens and it changes your whole life. If I didn't meet him, my whole life would have been different. I would have lived a life earning money, I guess. One with money as the focus, instead of a cause.

He didn't have any idea that he impacted me like that. He shook my hand and he almost cried, and really thanked me for listening to him.

He changed my whole attitude.

He changed my whole life.

Epilogue

In 2014, with the sounding of the gong, I stood up to participate in one more round of campaigning. I worked as an auxiliary arm of the central campaign to help re-elect Neil Abercrombie.

It's been five years since I had stepped down as executive director of HCEOC, and I had thought 2010 was my last political hurrah. I'd participated that year in the campaign to elect Congressman Neil Abercrombie for governor, in order to gain support for the mobilization of funds for our agency to operate programs for the poor.

He won in 2010 with a resounding victory and he went on to rack up an enviable record of accomplishments that no other Hawai'i governor ever matched.

He abolished Furlough Fridays, a practice requiring public employees to take Fridays off without pay, which the previous administration had imposed, and re-established a regular work week. Two years into his administration, government employees received higher pay and benefit increases than they had bargained for.

Though he inherited a state budget deficit of more than $200 million when he took office, within three years, state revenues increased to one billion dollars, the first hefty increase in the history of this state

He inherited a bankrupt Unemployment Trust Fund; today it has more than $300 million in reserve.

He released more than $420 million for Big Island construction projects to create jobs and stimulate economic activities and for education and human service programs; the Big Island's unemployment rate was reduced from more than nine percent to six percent.

Neil Abercrombie is sometimes perceived to be arrogant and contemptuous, but in reality he is that way only to the extent of emphasizing a point. His only recreation is lifting weights at the YMCA, and then he is back to work again. He thrives in working tirelessly at difficult tasks.

The 2014 campaign for incumbent Governor Neil Abercrombie started out as business as usual with the majority of our campaign team comprised of members from the previous campaign, which had won all seven districts of our county in a landslide victory. But sadly, in an atmosphere of overconfidence, though faced with a predicament of the urgency for a campaign, complacency set in.

A Big Island rolling poll survey foretold a disastrous outcome. The first poll showed Abercrombie ahead by five percent, the second tally by three percent, and then the tallies of the third to the seventh indicated a consistent loss ending with thirty-eight percent of the vote for incumbent Abercrombie and fifty-six percent for the challenger David Ige.

A statewide poll also showed Abercrombie losing in each county. Alas, he was indeed soundly defeated by State Senator Ige in the primary election throughout the state.

Regrettably and unfortunately, in its capriciousness, the voting public ignored Governor Abercrombie's many accomplishments and voted to unseat him.

Being a Democrat, though, I will support David Ige for governor in the 2014 General Election.

With Abercrombie's defeat, I realized that within just the five years since I stepped down from the executive director's position, the grassroots power we'd relied upon so much—held together by a spirit of devotion and enthusiasm for more than forty years—had diminished. Many experienced members had retired or passed away, and our grassroots membership had dwindled. I was no longer a critical cog who could recruit and rally the troops, as I'd done in prior elections. I could only provide support to the remnants of our grassroots on a small scale.

Looking back, I must admit that work and play became synonymous. I had fun, and am still enjoying my work of mobilizing resources for programs for the poor. Time flies by, as it always does, and as always some good things come to an end. But I know that new ones will come about.

PAU

www.ingramcontent.com/pod-product-compliance
Lightning Source LLC
Chambersburg PA
CBHW061318040426
42444CB00011B/2701